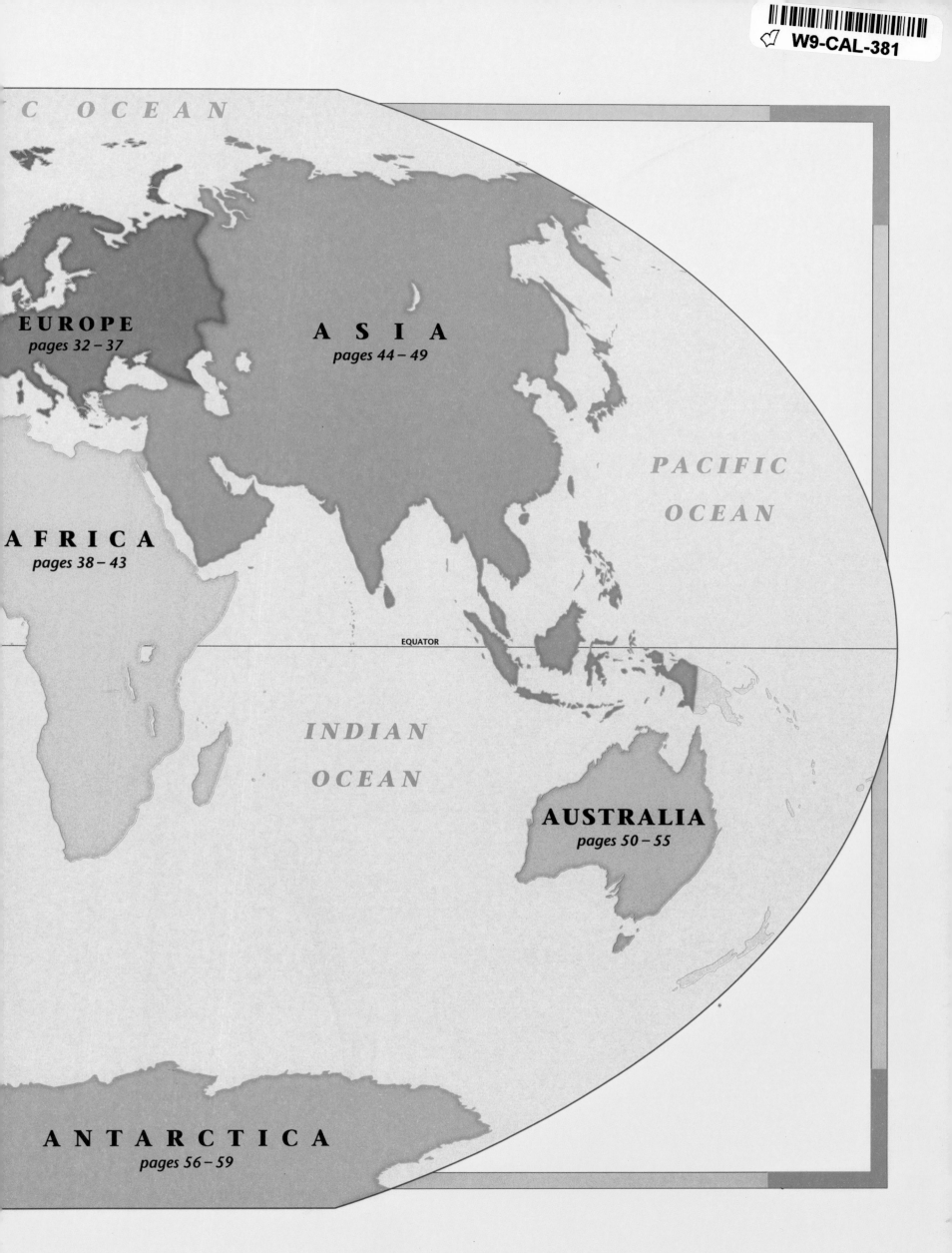

C OCEAN

EUROPE
*pages 32 – 37*

A S I A
*pages 44 – 49*

PACIFIC

OCEAN

AFRICA
*pages 38 – 43*

EQUATOR

INDIAN

OCEAN

AUSTRALIA
*pages 50 – 55*

A N T A R C T I C A
*pages 56 – 59*

NATIONAL GEOGRAPHIC

# BEGINNER'S
# World
# Atlas

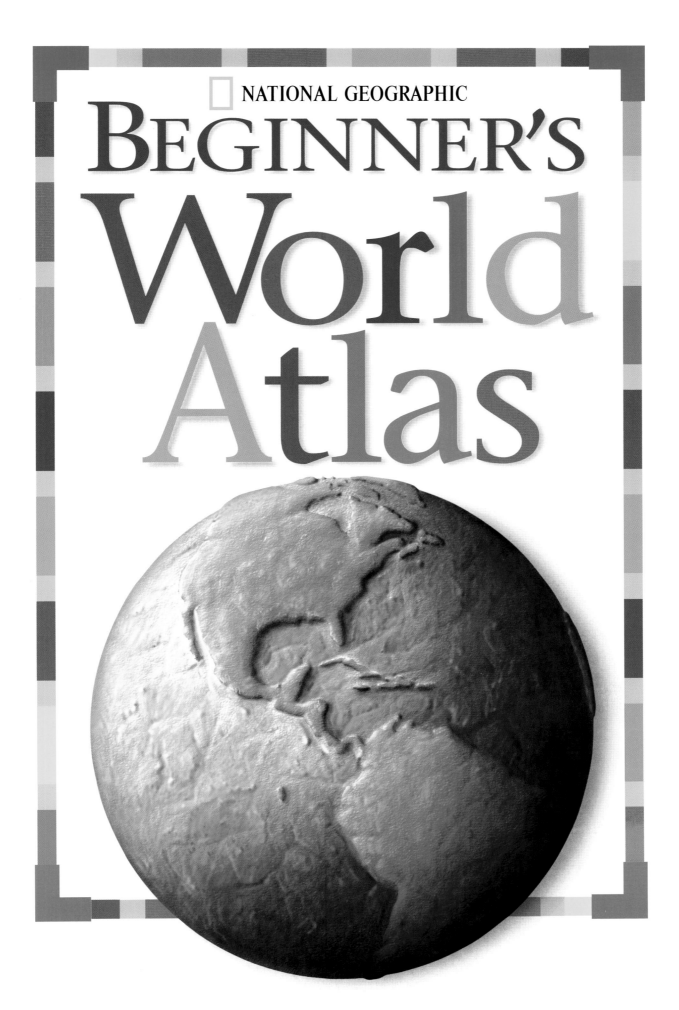

NATIONAL GEOGRAPHIC SOCIETY
WASHINGTON, D.C.

*Photographs from Tony Stone Images*

NATIONAL GEOGRAPHIC

# Beginner's World Atlas

## Table of Contents

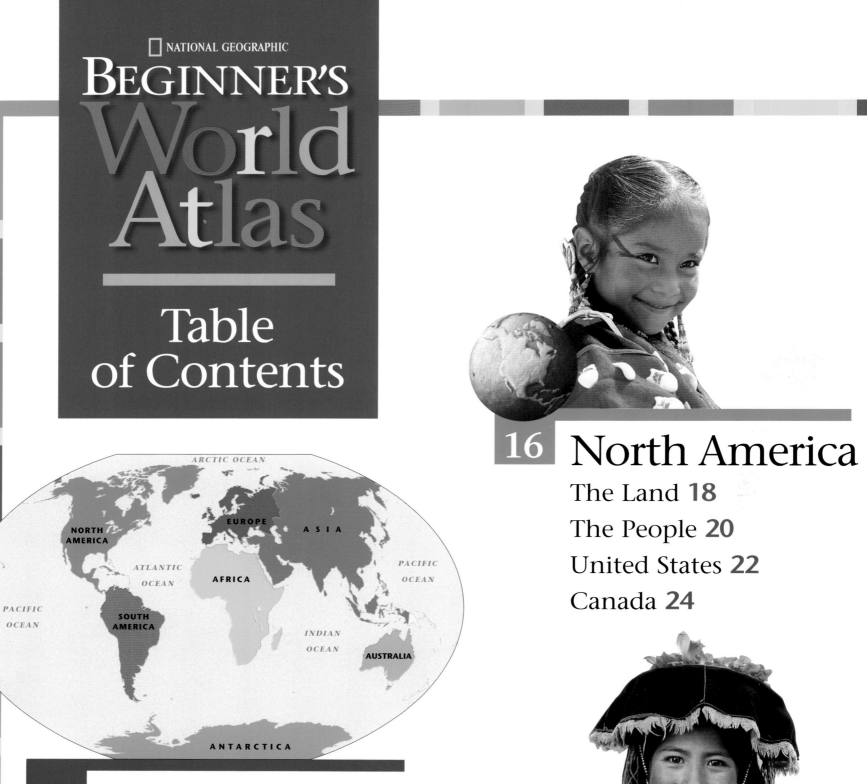

# What Is a Map?

**A** map is a drawing of a place as it looks from above. It is flat, and it is smaller than the place it shows. A map can help you find where you are and where you want to go.

## Mapping Your Backyard...

### ...from the ground

From your backyard you see everything in front of you straight on. You have to look up to see your roof and the tops of trees. You can't see what's in front of your house.

### ...from higher up

From higher up you look down on things. You can see the tops of trees and things in your yard and in the yards of other houses in your neighborhood.

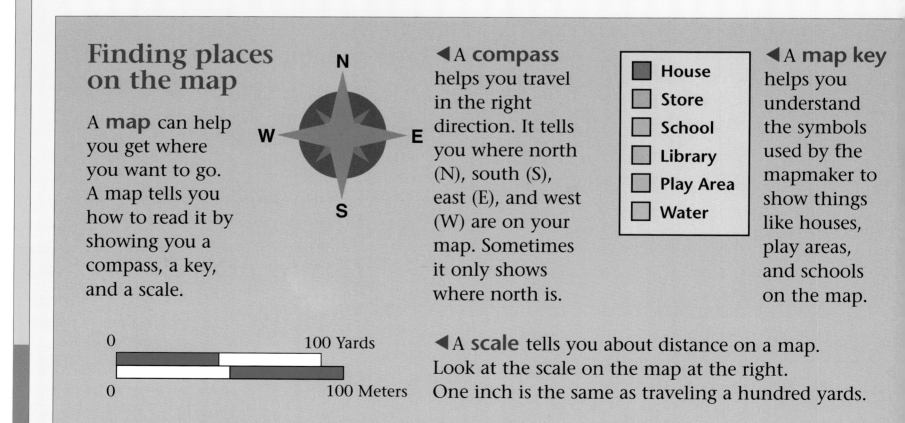

## Finding places on the map

A **map** can help you get where you want to go. A map tells you how to read it by showing you a compass, a key, and a scale.

◄A **compass** helps you travel in the right direction. It tells you where north (N), south (S), east (E), and west (W) are on your map. Sometimes it only shows where north is.

**House**
**Store**
**School**
**Library**
**Play Area**
**Water**

◄A **map key** helps you understand the symbols used by the mapmaker to show things like houses, play areas, and schools on the map.

0      100 Yards

0      100 Meters

◄A **scale** tells you about distance on a map. Look at the scale on the map at the right. One inch is the same as traveling a hundred yards.

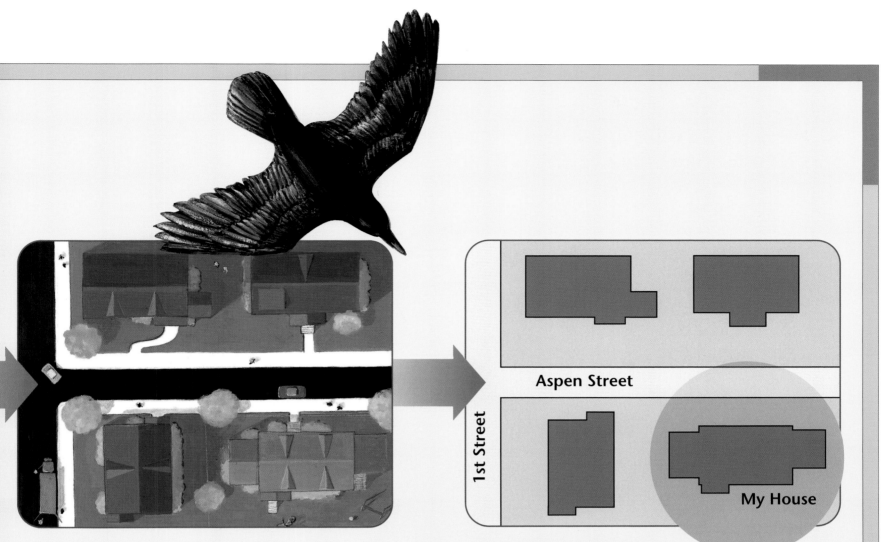

## ...from a bird's-eye view

If you were a bird flying directly overhead, you would only see the tops of things. You wouldn't see walls, tree trunks, tires, or feet.

## ...on a map

A map looks at places from a bird's-eye view. But it uses drawings called symbols to show things like houses that don't move.

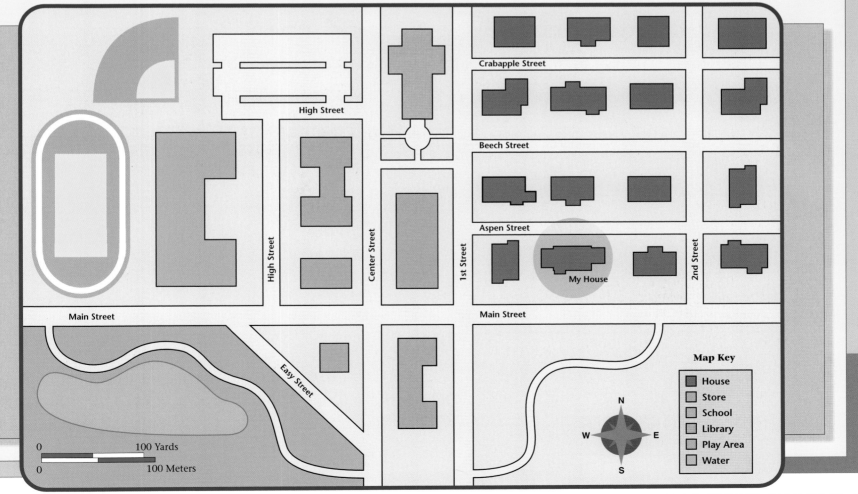

**Map Key**
- House
- Store
- School
- Library
- Play Area
- Water

# Making the Round Earth Flat

From your backyard the Earth probably looks flat. If you could travel into space like an astronaut, you would see that Earth is a giant ball with blue oceans, greenish-brown land, and white clouds. Even in space you can only see the part of Earth facing you. To see the whole Earth at one time you need a map. Maps take the round Earth and make it flat so you can see all of it at one time.

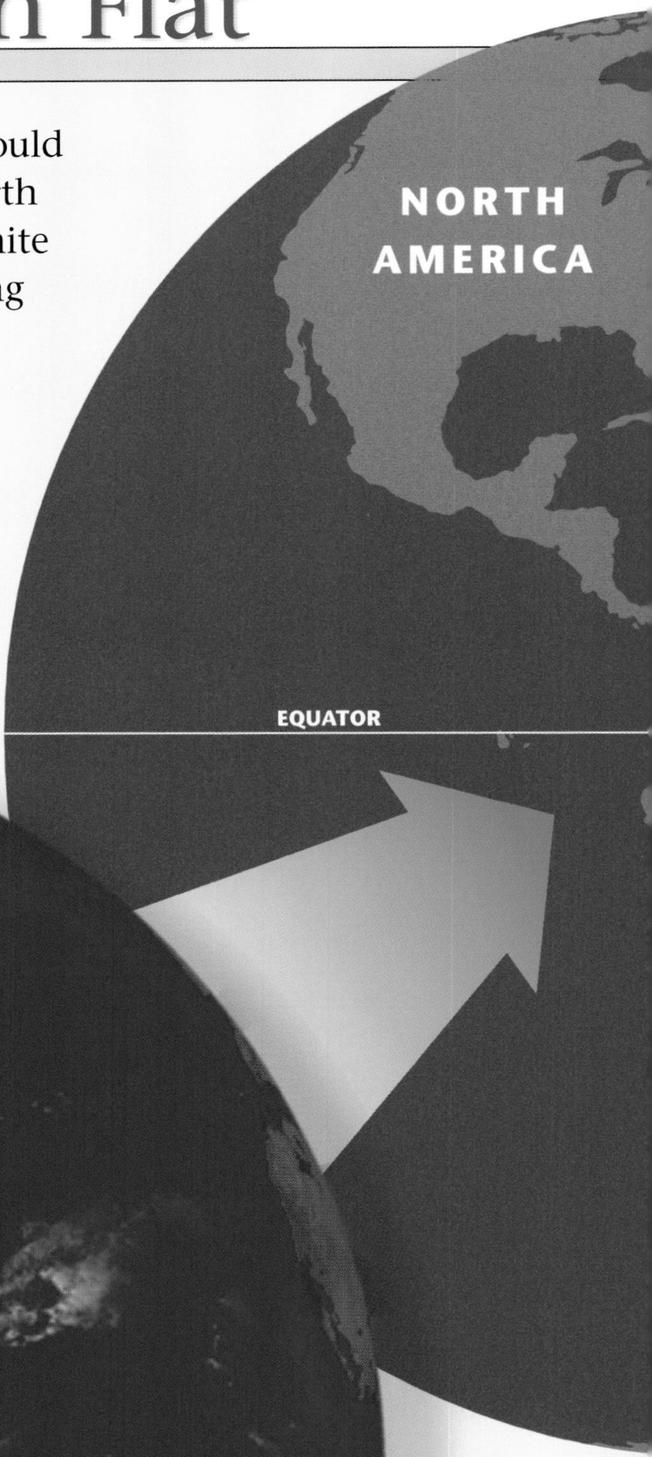

## ▼ Earth in Space

From space you can see that the Earth is round with oceans, land, and clouds. But you can see only half the Earth at one time.

NORTH
AMERICA

EQUATOR

**SOUTH AMERICA**

## ▲ Earth as a Globe

A **globe** is a tiny model of the Earth that you can put on a stand or hold in your hand. You have to turn it to see the other side. You still can't see the whole Earth at one time.

The **Equator** is an imaginary line around the middle of the Earth. Mapmakers show it as a solid or a dashed line on globes and maps.

## ▼ Earth on Paper

If you could peel a globe like an orange, you could make the Earth flat, but there would be spaces between the pieces. Mapmakers stretch the land and the water at the top and bottom to fill in the spaces. This is how a **map** lets you see the whole world all at once.

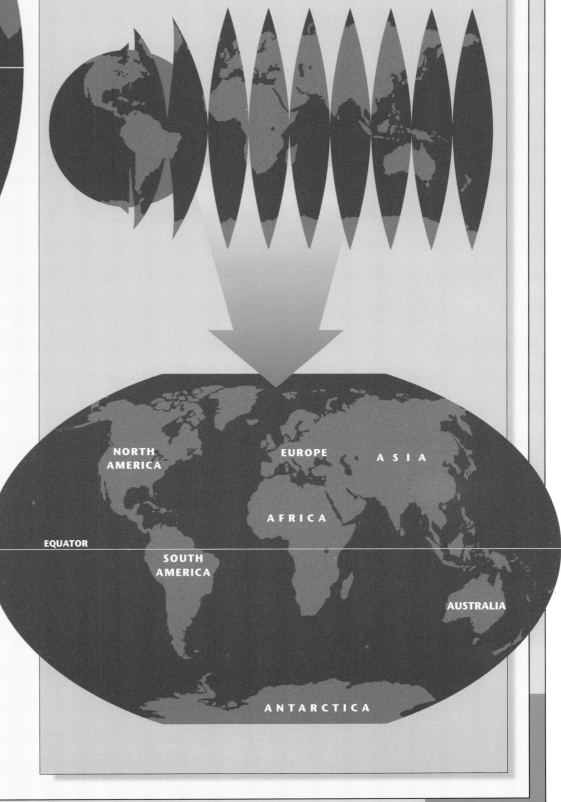

NORTH AMERICA

EUROPE

ASIA

AFRICA

EQUATOR

SOUTH AMERICA

AUSTRALIA

ANTARCTICA

# The Physical World

A physical map uses symbols to show where mountains, deserts, forests, and other features of the land are. The map key tells what the symbols mean.

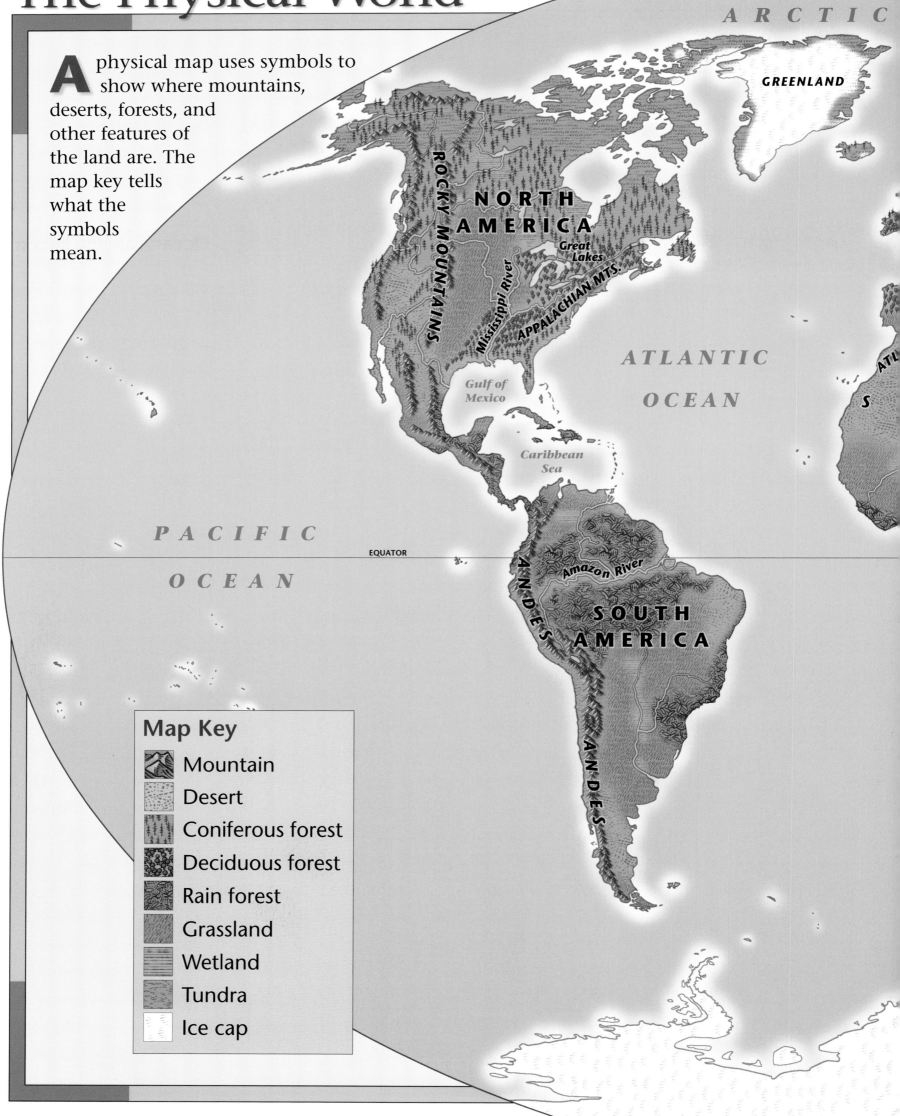

ARCTIC

GREENLAND

NORTH AMERICA

ROCKY MOUNTAINS

Great Lakes

Mississippi River

APPALACHIAN MTS.

ATLANTIC OCEAN

Gulf of Mexico

Caribbean Sea

PACIFIC OCEAN

EQUATOR

ANDES

Amazon River

SOUTH AMERICA

## Map Key

- Mountain
- Desert
- Coniferous forest
- Deciduous forest
- Rain forest
- Grassland
- Wetland
- Tundra
- Ice cap

OCEAN

EUROPE

URAL MTS.

Volga River

Europe-Asia
boundary

ALPS

Mediterranean Sea

S.

A S I A

Gobi

HIMALAYA

Yangtze River

ARA

SA RA

AFRICA

Nile River

PACIFIC

OCEAN

EQUATOR

INDIAN

OCEAN

AUSTRALIA

GREAT DIVIDING RANGE

| 0 | | 2000 miles |
| --- | --- | --- |
| 0 | | 3000 kilometers |

ANTARCTICA

# The Physical World Close Up

The Earth's surface is made up of land and water. The biggest landmasses are called **continents**. All seven of them are named on this map. **Islands** are smaller pieces of land that are surrounded by water. Greenland is the largest island. Land that is nearly surrounded by water is called a **peninsula**. Europe has lots of them.

**Oceans** are the largest bodies of water. Can you find all four oceans? **Lakes** are bodies of water surrounded by land—like the Great Lakes, in North America. A large stream of water that flows into a lake or an ocean is called a **river**. The Nile is Earth's longest river.

These are Earth's main physical features. But continents also have mountains, deserts, forests, and many other kinds of physical features. The **map symbols** below show the features that will appear on the physical maps in this atlas. Each symbol is followed by a brief definition that explains the meaning of each symbol. There is also a photograph so you can see what each feature looks like in the real world.

Each continent has different kinds of features, so each physical map will have its own map key.

**Mountain**

Land that rises at least 1,000 feet above the surrounding land

**Desert**

Very dry land that can be hot or cold and sandy or rocky

**Coniferous forest**

Forest with trees that have seed cones and often needlelike leaves

## Ice cap
A permanent sheet of thick ice that covers the land, as in Antarctica

## Tundra
A cold region with low plants that grow during warm months

## Wetland
Land, such as a marsh or swamp, that is mostly covered with water

## Deciduous forest
Forest with trees that loose leaves in fall and grow new ones in spring

## Rain forest
Forest with trees that keep their leaves all year and need lots of rain

## Grassland
A grass-covered area with too little rain for many trees to grow

# The Political World

**P**olitical maps show places where people live. This one names the countries of the world. Colors make it easy to see the size and shape of each one.

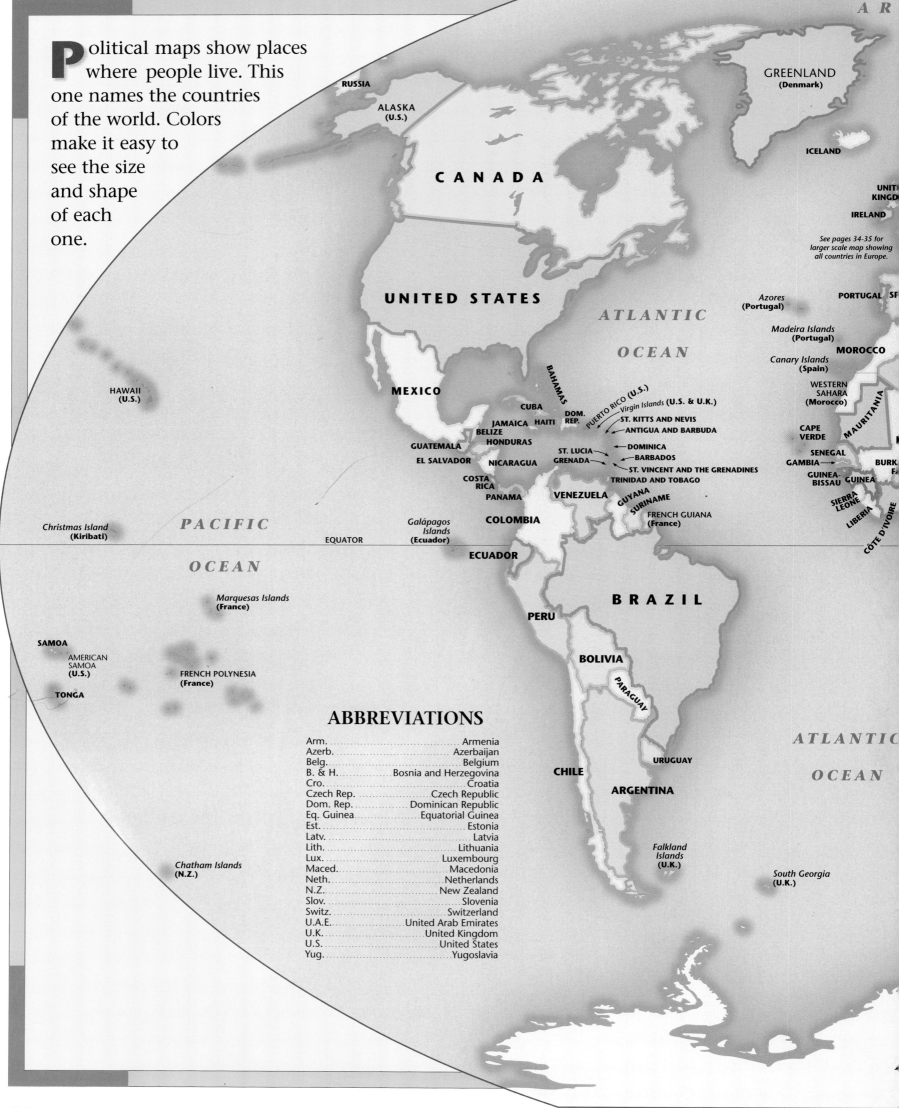

RUSSIA

ALASKA (U.S.)

CANADA

UNITED STATES

MEXICO

HAWAII (U.S.)

GUATEMALA
EL SALVADOR
BELIZE
HONDURAS
NICARAGUA
COSTA RICA
PANAMA

CUBA
JAMAICA  HAITI
DOM. REP.
PUERTO RICO (U.S.)
Virgin Islands (U.S. & U.K.)
ST. KITTS AND NEVIS
ANTIGUA AND BARBUDA
DOMINICA
ST. LUCIA
GRENADA
BARBADOS
ST. VINCENT AND THE GRENADINES
TRINIDAD AND TOBAGO

BAHAMAS

VENEZUELA
COLOMBIA
GUYANA
SURINAME
FRENCH GUIANA (France)

ECUADOR
Galápagos Islands (Ecuador)

Christmas Island (Kiribati)

PACIFIC

OCEAN

EQUATOR

ATLANTIC

OCEAN

GREENLAND (Denmark)

ICELAND

UNITED KINGDOM
IRELAND

*See pages 34-35 for larger scale map showing all countries in Europe.*

Azores (Portugal)

PORTUGAL  SPAIN

Madeira Islands (Portugal)

MOROCCO

Canary Islands (Spain)

WESTERN SAHARA (Morocco)

MAURITANIA

CAPE VERDE

SENEGAL
GAMBIA
GUINEA-BISSAU  GUINEA
SIERRA LEONE
LIBERIA
CÔTE D'IVOIRE
BURKINA FASO

BRAZIL

PERU

BOLIVIA

PARAGUAY

CHILE

URUGUAY

ARGENTINA

ATLANTIC

OCEAN

Marquesas Islands (France)

SAMOA
AMERICAN SAMOA (U.S.)
TONGA

FRENCH POLYNESIA (France)

Chatham Islands (N.Z.)

Falkland Islands (U.K.)

South Georgia (U.K.)

## ABBREVIATIONS

Arm. .......................................... Armenia
Azerb. ...................................... Azerbaijan
Belg. .......................................... Belgium
B. & H. .............. Bosnia and Herzegovina
Cro. ............................................ Croatia
Czech Rep. ......................... Czech Republic
Dom. Rep. ..................... Dominican Republic
Eq. Guinea .................... Equatorial Guinea
Est. ............................................. Estonia
Latv. ............................................. Latvia
Lith. .......................................... Lithuania
Lux. ....................................... Luxembourg
Maced. ..................................... Macedonia
Neth. ...................................... Netherlands
N.Z. ...................................... New Zealand
Slov. .......................................... Slovenia
Switz. ..................................... Switzerland
U.A.E. .................... United Arab Emirates
U.K. ................................... United Kingdom
U.S. ...................................... United States
Yug. ........................................ Yugoslavia

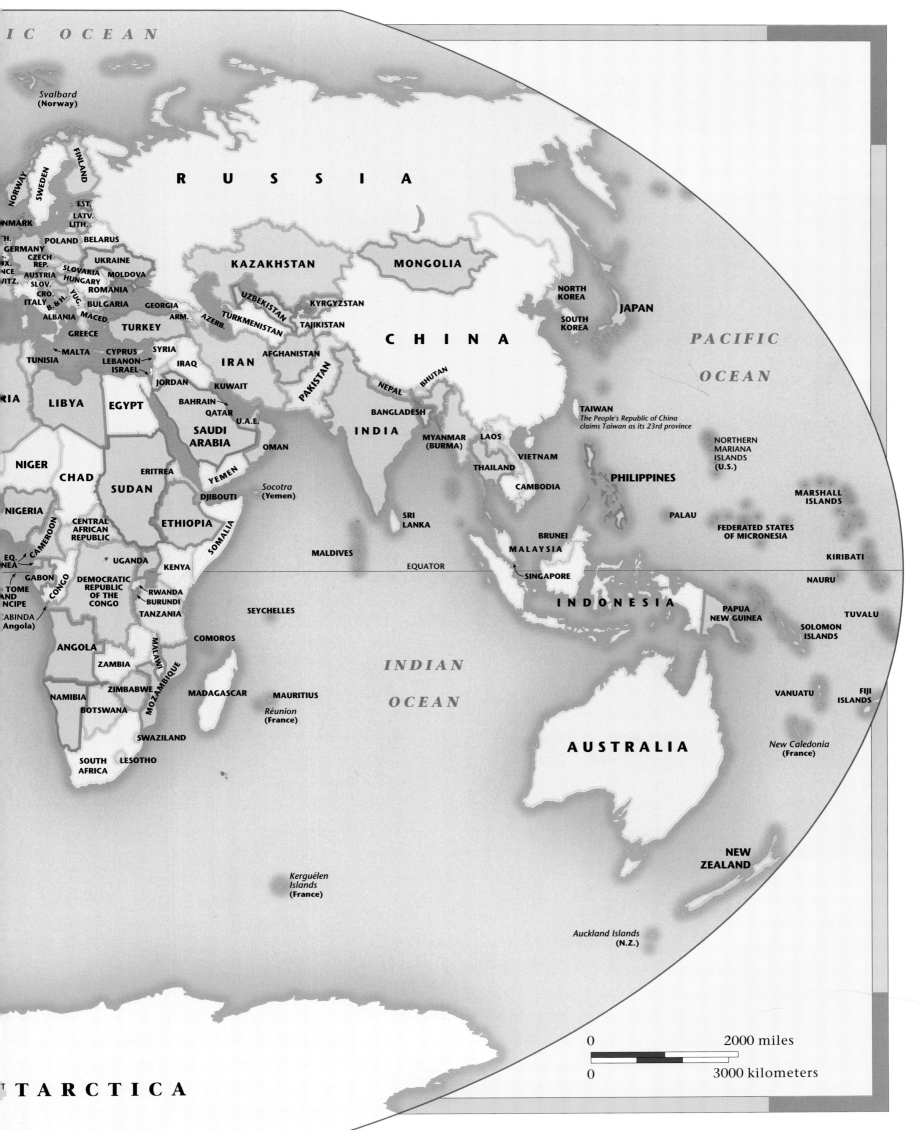

IC OCEAN

Svalbard
(Norway)

NORWAY
SWEDEN
FINLAND
EST.
LATV.
LITH.
NMARK
POLAND BELARUS
TH.
GERMANY
CZECH
REP.
NX.
ANCE
AUSTRIA
VITZ.
SLOV.
ITALY
B.&H.
YUG.
ALBANIA MACED.
GREECE
MALTA
TUNISIA
CYPRUS
LEBANON
ISRAEL

R U S S I A

KAZAKHSTAN

MONGOLIA

NORTH
KOREA

JAPAN

SOUTH
KOREA

UZBEKISTAN
KYRGYZSTAN

TURKMENISTAN
TAJIKISTAN

GEORGIA
ARM.
AZERB.

C H I N A

SLOVAKIA
HUNGARY
ROMANIA
BULGARIA
TURKEY

SYRIA
IRAQ
IRAN

AFGHANISTAN

PAKISTAN

NEPAL
BHUTAN

PACIFIC

OCEAN

TAIWAN
The People's Republic of China
claims Taiwan as its 23rd province

JORDAN
KUWAIT
BAHRAIN
QATAR
U.A.E.

RIA

LIBYA

EGYPT

SAUDI
ARABIA

OMAN

INDIA

BANGLADESH

MYANMAR
(BURMA)

LAOS

VIETNAM

NORTHERN
MARIANA
ISLANDS
(U.S.)

THAILAND

PHILIPPINES

NIGER

CHAD

SUDAN

ERITREA

YEMEN

Socotra
(Yemen)

CAMBODIA

MARSHALL
ISLANDS

NIGERIA

CENTRAL
AFRICAN
REPUBLIC

DJIBOUTI

ETHIOPIA

SRI
LANKA

PALAU

FEDERATED STATES
OF MICRONESIA

EQ.
NEA

CAMEROON

SOMALIA

MALDIVES

BRUNEI

KIRIBATI

GABON

UGANDA

KENYA

EQUATOR

MALAYSIA

SINGAPORE

NAURU

TOME
NCIPE

DEMOCRATIC
REPUBLIC
OF THE
CONGO

RWANDA
BURUNDI

ABINDA
Angola)

CONGO

TANZANIA

SEYCHELLES

I N D O N E S I A

PAPUA
NEW GUINEA

TUVALU

SOLOMON
ISLANDS

ANGOLA

ZAMBIA

COMOROS

INDIAN

NAMIBIA

ZIMBABWE

MALAWI

MOZAMBIQUE

MADAGASCAR

MAURITIUS

OCEAN

VANUATU

FIJI
ISLANDS

BOTSWANA

Réunion
(France)

SWAZILAND

SOUTH
AFRICA

LESOTHO

AUSTRALIA

New Caledonia
(France)

Kerguélen
Islands
(France)

NEW
ZEALAND

Auckland Islands
(N.Z.)

TARCTICA

0          2000 miles

0          3000 kilometers

# What This Atlas Will Teach You

**Y**ou hold the world in your hands as you look through the pages of this atlas. You will find a physical and a political map of each continent. Here is what you will learn about each one.

Coral reef, Pacific Ocean

Mountains, Asia

THE PHYSICAL WORLD

 **Land regions** You will find out what kinds of land cover a continent. Does it have mountains and deserts? If so, where are they?

 **Water** You will learn about a continent's chief lakes, rivers, and waterfalls. You'll see that some continents have more water than others.

 **Climate** Climate is the weather of a place over many years. Some continents are colder and wetter or hotter and drier than others.

**Plants** You'll discover what kinds of plants grow on a particular continent.

Desert, North America

**Animals** Continents each have certain kinds of animals. Did you know that tigers live in the wild only in Asia?

Camels, Asia

Vancouver, Canada

Grapes, Mediterranean region

Eiffel Tower, France

ARCTIC OCEAN

GREENLAND (Denmark)

NORWAY
ICELAND    FINLAND    R U S S I A
CANADA    UNITED KINGDOM
UKRAINE    KAZAKHSTAN    MONGOLIA
FRANCE
UNITED STATES    SPAIN    TURKEY    JAPAN
SYRIA    IRAN    CHINA    PACIFIC OCEAN
MOROCCO    EGYPT
MEXICO    ALGERIA    LIBYA    SAUDI ARABIA    INDIA
CUBA    MAURITANIA    MALI    NIGER    CHAD    SUDAN    THAILAND    VIETNAM
VENEZUELA    PHILIPPINES
NICARAGUA    GUYANA    ETHIOPIA
COLOMBIA    SURINAME    LIBERIA    NIGERIA    SOMALIA
PACIFIC OCEAN    ECUADOR    DEMOCRATIC REPUBLIC OF THE CONGO    TANZANIA    EQUATOR    INDONESIA    PAPUA NEW GUINEA
PERU    BRAZIL    ANGOLA    ZAMBIA
BOLIVIA    MADAGASCAR
PARAGUAY    NAMIBIA    INDIAN OCEAN
CHILE    URUGUAY    SOUTH AFRICA    AUSTRALIA
ARGENTINA    OCEAN    NEW ZEALAND

ATLANTIC OCEAN

ANTARCTICA

## THE POLITICAL WORLD

**Countries** You will learn about the countries that make up a continent. Maps show country names in type like this: **UNITED STATES**

**Cities** You will find out which are the most important cities on a continent. The map key will tell you which cities are country capitals.

**People** You will learn where groups of people on a continent come from, where they live, what they do, how they have fun, and more.

**Languages** Many languages are spoken on most continents. Here you will find out which ones most people speak.

**Products** This section will tell you which goods produced on a continent are most important to the people living there.

Eurostar train, Europe

Schoolgirls, Vietnam

# North America

**N**orth America is shaped like a triangle ▼. It is wide in the north. In the south it narrows to a strip of land so narrow that a Marathon runner could cross it in two hours. Ships make the trip on the Panama Canal. The warm islands in the Caribbean Sea are part of North America. So is icy Greenland in the far north. The seven countries between Mexico and South America make up a region commonly called Central America. It connects the rest of North America and South America.

Kha-hay! I'm from the Crow tribe in Montana. This beautiful valley is in Yosemite National Park, in California. It's in the Sierra Nevada mountains. Look for them on the map when you turn the page.

# North America

## The Land

![mountains icon] **Land regions** The Rocky Mountains run along the west side of North America through Mexico. There, the mountains are called the Sierra Madre Oriental. Lower mountains called the Appalachians are in the east. Grassy plains lie between the two mountain chains.

![water icon] **Water** The longest rivers are the Mississippi and the Missouri. The Great Lakes are the world's largest group of freshwater lakes.

![climate icon] **Climate** The far north is icy cold. Temperatures get warmer as you move south. Much of Central America is hot and wet.

![plants icon] **Plants** North America has large forests where there is plenty of rain. Grasslands cover drier areas.

![animals icon] **Animals** There is a big variety of animals—everything from bears, moose, and wolves to monkeys and colorful parrots.

*Mt. McKinley (Denali)*
*Highest elevation in North America*

▲ North America is famous for its **deciduous forests**. Leaves turn fiery colors each fall!

▲ A white-tail deer nuzzles her babies in a meadow near the **Great Lakes**. Deer live in almost every country on the continent.

◀ Palm trees grow along sandy beaches on islands in the **Caribbean Sea**. In this part of North America the weather is warm year-round.

◀ Dragonlike iguanas live in the **rain forests** of Mexico and Central America. This harmless lizard can grow as long as a man's leg.

▼ **Deserts** are found in the southwestern part of North America. The large rock formation on the right is called The Mitten. Can you guess why?

ASIA

ARCTIC
OCEAN

GREENLAND

Brooks Range

Yukon River

Mackenzie River

Great
Bear Lake

Great
Slave Lake

Hudson
Bay

R O C K Y   M O U N T A I N S

Columbia River

Sierra Nevada

G R E A T   P L A I N S

Missouri River

Lake
Winnipeg

Great Lakes

Colorado River

Death Valley
Lowest elevation in
North America

Rio Grande

Mississippi River

Ohio River

Appalachian Mountains

ATLANTIC
OCEAN

PACIFIC
OCEAN

SIERRA MADRE OCCIDENTAL

SIERRA MADRE ORIENTAL

Gulf of Mexico

W E S T   I N D I E S

CENTRAL AMERICA

Caribbean Sea

SOUTH AMERICA

▲ This view from
a plane shows that
**Greenland** has high
mountains and lots
of snow and ice.

## Map Key

Mountain
Desert
Coniferous forest
Deciduous forest
Rain forest
Grassland
Wetland
Tundra
Ice cap

0        600 miles

0        900 kilometers

# North America

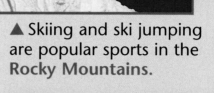

## The People

 **Countries** Canada, the United States, Mexico, and the countries of Central America and the West Indies make up North America.

▲ Skiing and ski jumping are popular sports in the **Rocky Mountains**.

 **Cities** Mexico City is the biggest city in North America. Next in size are New York City and Los Angeles. Havana, in Cuba, is the largest city in the West Indies.

▲ This farmer is harvesting wheat on a big farm in **Canada**. Canada and the United States grow much of the world's wheat.

**People** The ancestors of most people in North America came from Europe. Many other people trace their roots to Africa and Asia. Native Americans live throughout.

**Languages** English and Spanish are the main languages. A large number of people in Canada and Haiti speak French. There are also many Native American languages.

▲ This pyramid at **Chichén Itzá** was built long ago by the Maya people.

**Products** North America's chief products include cars, machinery, petroleum, natural gas, silver, wheat, corn, beef, and forest products.

◄ These red berries hold coffee beans. Many farmers in **Guatemala** make a living growing coffee.

▲ This is **Mexico City**. More people live here than in any other city in North America.

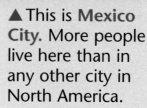

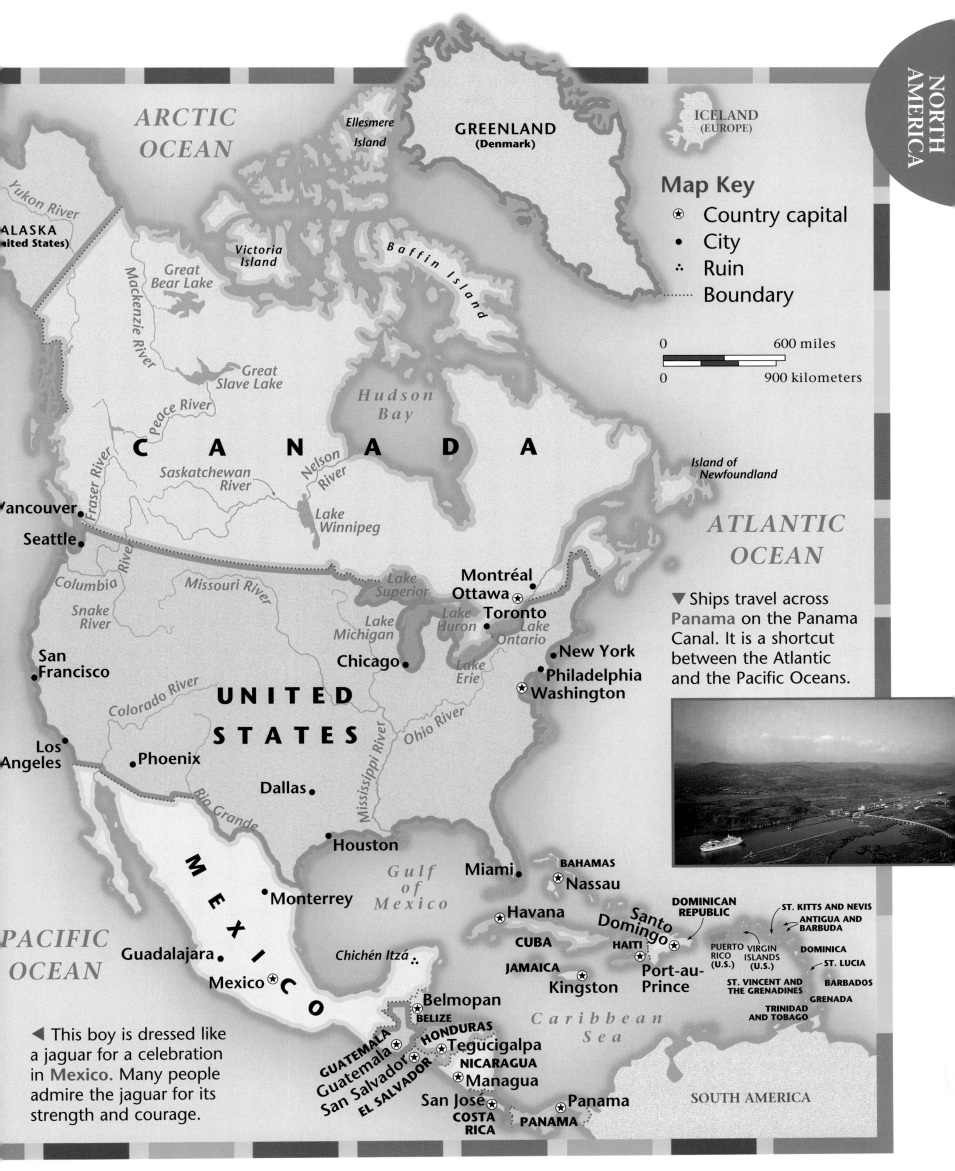

*ARCTIC OCEAN*

Ellesmere Island

GREENLAND (Denmark)

ICELAND (EUROPE)

*Yukon River*

ALASKA (United States)

Victoria Island

*Baffin Island*

## Map Key

⊛  Country capital
•  City
∴  Ruin
·······  Boundary

0          600 miles
0          900 kilometers

*Great Bear Lake*

*Mackenzie River*

*Great Slave Lake*

*Peace River*

*Hudson Bay*

C A N A D A

*Saskatchewan River*

*Nelson River*

*Fraser River*

Island of Newfoundland

*ATLANTIC OCEAN*

Vancouver

Seattle

River

*Lake Winnipeg*

*Columbia River*

*Missouri River*

*Lake Superior*

Montréal
Ottawa ⊛
Toronto

▼ Ships travel across **Panama** on the Panama Canal. It is a shortcut between the Atlantic and the Pacific Oceans.

*Snake River*

San Francisco

*Lake Michigan*

*Lake Huron*

*Lake Ontario*

Chicago

*Lake Erie*

New York
Philadelphia
⊛ Washington

U N I T E D   S T A T E S

*Colorado River*

*Ohio River*

Los Angeles

Phoenix

*Mississippi River*

Dallas

*Rio Grande*

Houston

*PACIFIC OCEAN*

M E X I C O

Monterrey

*Gulf of Mexico*

Miami

BAHAMAS
⊛ Nassau

DOMINICAN REPUBLIC

ST. KITTS AND NEVIS
ANTIGUA AND BARBUDA

Guadalajara

*Chichén Itzá* ∴

⊛ Havana

Santo Domingo ⊛

Mexico ⊛

CUBA

HAITI

PUERTO RICO (U.S.)

VIRGIN ISLANDS (U.S.)

DOMINICA

ST. LUCIA

JAMAICA

⊛ Port-au-Prince

◄ This boy is dressed like a jaguar for a celebration in **Mexico**. Many people admire the jaguar for its strength and courage.

Belmopan ⊛
BELIZE

Kingston

ST. VINCENT AND THE GRENADINES

BARBADOS

GRENADA

*Caribbean Sea*

TRINIDAD AND TOBAGO

GUATEMALA
Guatemala ⊛
San Salvador ⊛
EL SALVADOR

HONDURAS
Tegucigalpa ⊛
NICARAGUA
⊛ Managua

San José ⊛
COSTA RICA

⊛ Panama
PANAMA

SOUTH AMERICA

# United States

## The People

 **States** The United States is made up of 50 states. Alaska and Hawaii are separated from the rest of the country. So you can see them close up, they are shown near the bottom of the map. Use the small globe to see their real locations.

▲ Chinese New Year is a big celebration in San Francisco. Lots of Chinese live there.

**Cities** Washington, D.C., is the national capital. Each state also has a capital city. New York City has the most people.

**People** People from almost every country in the world live in the United States. Most live and work in and around cities.

▲ Sandy beaches, like this one in Delaware, are popular places to visit in the summer.

**Languages** English is the chief language, followed by Spanish.

**Products** The chief products include cars, machinery, petroleum, natural gas, coal, beef, wheat, and forest products.

▶ Soccer is a popular sport in the United States along with baseball, basketball, and football. Many children join teams at an early age.

Seattle
Olympia
WASHINGTON
Portland
Salem
OREGON
IDAHO
Boise
Columbia River
Sacramento
San Francisco
San Jose
CALIFORNIA
Carson City
NEVADA
Salt Lake City
Las Vegas
Los Angeles
San Diego
ARIZONA
Phoenix
Tucson
PACIFIC OCEAN
ALASKA
Juneau
0    400 miles
0    600 kilometers
Honolulu
HAWAII
0    150 miles
0    200 kilometers

CANADA

Missouri River

MONTANA
• Helena

NORTH DAKOTA
⊙ Bismarck

MINNESOTA

Lake Superior

MAINE
⊙ Augusta

WYOMING

SOUTH DAKOTA
⊙ Pierre

Minneapolis •⊙ St. Paul
WISCONSIN
• Milwaukee
Madison ⊙

M I C H I G A N

L. Huron

Lake Ontario

Montpelier
VT. N.H.
⊙ Concord

NEW YORK
Albany ⊙ • Boston
Rochester • • Buffalo    Hartford ⊙ • Providence
MASS.
CONN. RHODE ISLAND

Cheyenne

NEBRASKA

Omaha •
Lincoln ⊙

I O W A
⊙ Des Moines

• Lansing

L. Michigan

• Detroit

L. Erie

Cleveland •
Pittsburgh •

PENNSYLVANIA
Harrisburg ⊙
Trenton

• New York
NEW JERSEY
• Philadelphia

Colorado River

Denver ⊙
COLORADO

ILLINOIS
Springfield ⊙

• Chicago

INDIANA
Indianapolis ⊙

OHIO
⊙ Columbus

Baltimore •
MARYLAND

Dover
DELAWARE
⊙ Annapolis
Washington,

Santa Fe ⊙

Topeka ⊙ •⊙ Kansas City
KANSAS    Jefferson City
Wichita •

• St. Louis

MISSOURI

Cincinnati •

Frankfort ⊙

KENTUCKY

WEST VIRGINIA
⊙ Charleston

D.C.
• Richmond

VIRGINIA

Raleigh •

• Albuquerque
NEW MEXICO

Tulsa •
OKLAHOMA
Oklahoma City ⊙

ARKANSAS
Little Rock ⊙

Memphis •

TENNESSEE

• Nashville

NORTH CAROLINA
• Charlotte

SOUTH
⊙ Columbia
CAROLINA

• El Paso

Forth Worth • • Dallas

Jackson ⊙

MISSISSIPPI

Atlanta ⊙
• Birmingham
ALABAMA    GEORGIA
⊙ Montgomery

• Savannah

TEXAS
Austin ⊙

LOUISIANA

Baton Rouge ⊙
• New Orleans

Mississippi River

Tallahassee ⊙

F L O R I D A

• Jacksonville

Houston •
• San Antonio

Rio Grande

Orlando •

Tampa •

• Miami

Gulf of Mexico

MEXICO

▲ This bridge is in **New York City**. The Empire State Building stands tall against the sky.

## Map Key

⊛ Country capital

⊙ State capital

• City

⋯ Boundary

0                400 miles

0                600 kilometers

◀ A scarecrow stands guard over a field of sunflowers in **Kansas**.

▶ Spicy boiled crawfish are a favorite dish in **Mississippi** and other states that border the Gulf of Mexico.

# Canada

## The People

**Provinces** Canada is divided into ten provinces and three territories. Nunavut is a brand-new homeland for Eskimos. The largest number of people live in Ontario and Quebec.

**Cities** Ottawa is Canada's capital. Toronto, Montreal, and Vancouver are among its largest cities and ports.

**People** Canada has fewer people than the state of California. Most Canadians live within a hundred miles of the country's southern border. The territories have a lot of land but very few people.

**Languages** Canada's street signs are often in two languages. That's because English and French are the chief languages. Most French-speaking Canadians live in Quebec.

**Products** Canada's chief products include cars, forest products, petroleum, natural gas, aluminum, nickel, iron ore, beef, and wheat.

▲ Royal Canadian Mounted Police often perform their famous Musical Ride in **Ottawa**.

▲ Banff, in **Alberta**, is one of several national parks in the Rocky Mountains of western Canada.

ARCTIC O

*Beaufort Sea*

ALASKA (U.S.)

YUKON TERRITORY

Mackenzie River

Great Bear Lak

Yukon River

⊙ Whitehorse    NORTHW TERRITO

Yellowknif

BRITISH COLUMBIA

Peace River

ALBERT

Fraser River

Edmonton ⊙

Vancouver Island

Victoria ⊙    ⊙ Vancouver    Calga

*PACIFIC OCEAN*

▼ During Canada's long, cold winters, ice hockey is a popular sport. The Hockey Hall of Fame is in **Toronto**, Ontario.

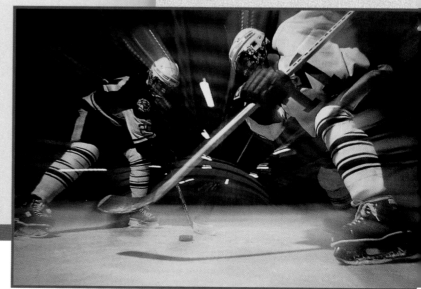

► The CN Tower rises high above Toronto's skyline. The city is a busy port on Lake Ontario.

*Queen Elizabeth Islands*

*Baffin Bay*

GREENLAND (DENMARK)

*Victoria Island*

NUNAVUT

*Baffin Island*

Iqaluit ◉

*Labrador Sea*

▲ Trains carry goods to every province and territory except one— Prince Edward Island.

*Great ve Lake*

ANADA

*Lake habasca*

*Hudson Bay*

NEWFOUNDLAND

Churchill ●

*Nelson River*

*St. John's* ◉

*Island of Newfoundland*

QUEBEC

KATCHEWAN   MANITOBA

*atchewan River*

*Lake Winnipeg*

ATLANTIC OCEAN

ONTARIO

Regina ◉

Winnipeg ◉

PRINCE EDWARD ISLAND

NEW BRUNSWICK

Charlottetown ◉

NOVA SCOTIA

UNITED STATES

*Lake Superior*

Québec ◉

Fredericton ◉   Halifax ◉

*St. Lawrence River*

Montréal ●

▼ Polar bears bring tourists to Churchill, Manitoba, a town on Hudson Bay.

Ottawa ★

*L. Huron*

*Lake Michigan*

Toronto ◉

*Lake Ontario*

Windsor ●

*L. Erie*

## Map Key

⊛ Country capital
◉ Province capital
● City
‧‧‧‧ Boundary

0            300 miles

0            400 kilometers

# South America

V isit South America, and you will see many wonderful things. It has the world's biggest rain forest and one of the driest deserts. It has emerald mines, mysterious ruins, and crowded modern cities with glass-and-steel skyscrapers. In the mountains, camel-like animals called llamas are trained to carry goods. On the grasslands, cowboys called gauchos round up cattle. You might be surprised to learn that some familiar foods, such as potatoes and tomatoes, are native to South America.

Imaynalla! Greetings in Quechua, my native language. I live in the mountains of Peru. Do you like my market-day outfit? Behind me is Iguazú Falls, one of the world's largest waterfalls. It's on the border between Argentina and Brazil.

# South America

## The Land

 **Land regions** Snowcapped mountains called the Andes run along the whole west coast. Rain forests and grasslands cover much of the rest of the continent. The driest desert lies between the Andes and the Pacific Ocean.

**Water** The Amazon River carries more water than any other river in the world. More than 1,000 streams and rivers flow into it. Lake Titicaca, in the Andes, is the continent's largest lake.

**Climate** Much of South America is warm all year. The coldest places are in the Andes and at the continent's southern tip. Each year about 80 inches of rain falls in the rain forests.

**Plants** The Amazon rain forest has more kinds of plants than any other place in the world. Grasslands feed large herds of cattle and sheep.

 **Animals** Colorful macaws, noisy howler monkeys, and giant snakes live in the rain forest. Sure-footed llamas, huge birds called condors, and guinea pigs live in the Andes. The flightless rhea, which looks like an ostrich, roams the southern grasslands.

▲ Cold outside and hot inside, snow-covered **volcanoes** are scattered through the Andes.

▶ The world's largest water lilies grow in the **Amazon River.** They are big enough to hold a child.

▲ The **Atacama,** in northern Chile, is one of the world's driest deserts.

▼ Imagine living in a place where birds are as big and as colorful as these macaws. They live in the **rain forest.**

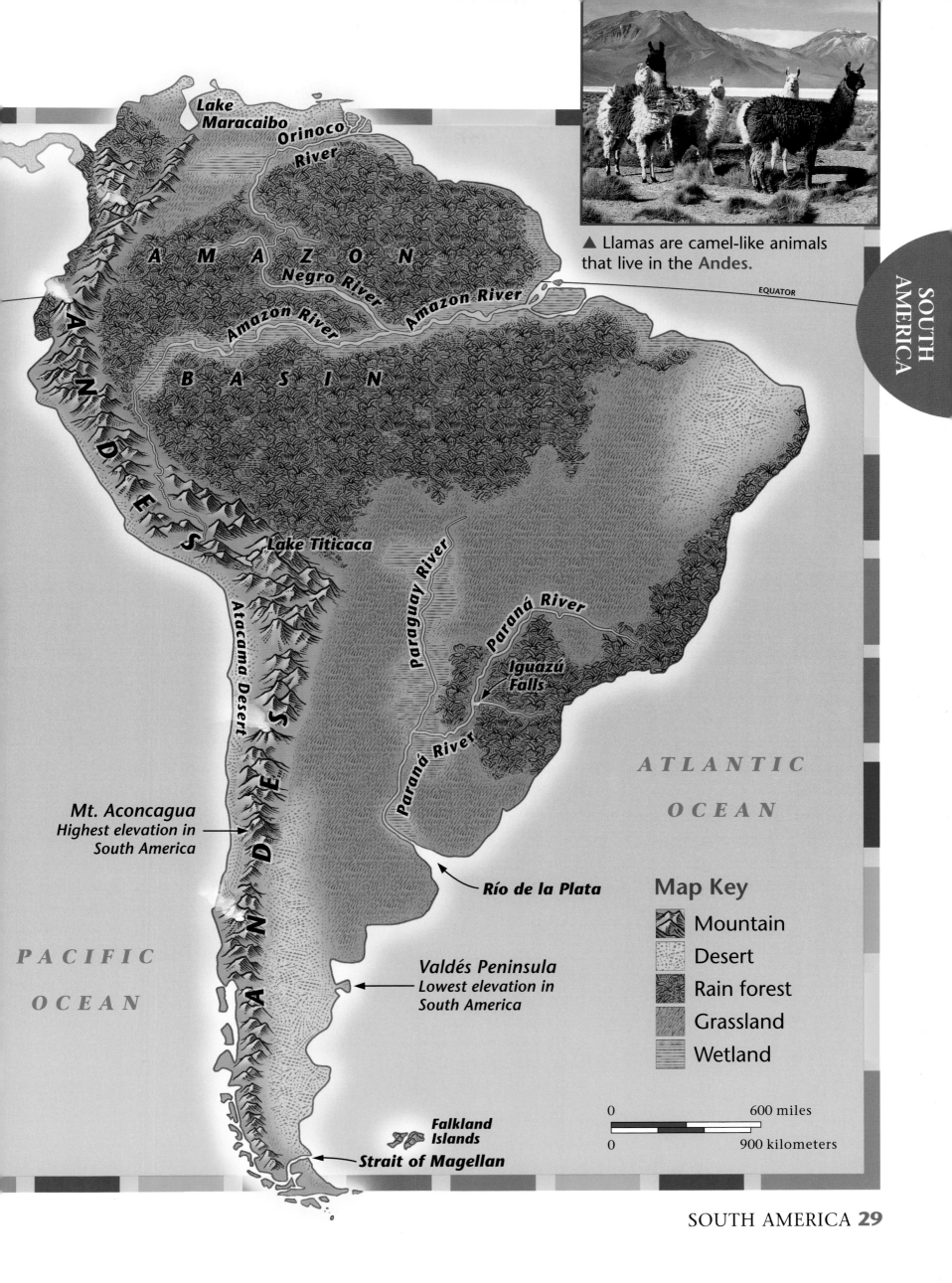

Lake Maracaibo

Orinoco River

A M A Z O N

Negro River

Amazon River

Amazon River

EQUATOR

B A S I N

A N D E S

Lake Titicaca

Paraguay River

Paraná River

Iguazú Falls

Atacama Desert

Mt. Aconcagua
*Highest elevation in South America*

Paraná River

ATLANTIC

OCEAN

Río de la Plata

PACIFIC

OCEAN

*Valdés Peninsula*
*Lowest elevation in South America*

Falkland Islands

Strait of Magellan

▲ Llamas are camel-like animals that live in the **Andes.**

## Map Key

Mountain

Desert

Rain forest

Grassland

Wetland

0      600 miles

0      900 kilometers

# South America

## The People

**Countries** South America has just 12 countries—French Guiana is not really a country because it belongs to France. All but two of these countries border an ocean. Can you find these two countries on the map?

**Cities** Most of the largest cities are near the oceans. São Paulo, in Brazil, is South America's biggest city. Bolivia has two capital cities: La Paz and Sucre.

**People** The native people came from the north long ago. Colonists came from Spain and Portugal. They brought Africans to work in the fields as slaves. Descendants of these three groups make up most of the people of South America.

**Languages** Spanish and Portuguese are the continent's chief languages. Indians speak Quechua and other native languages.

**Products** South America's chief products include bananas, cattle, coffee, copper, emeralds, oranges, and sugar.

◄ Many bananas sold in the United States and other countries come from **Ecuador**. Check the label the next time you go to the store!

▲ Long ago, the Inca people built the city of **Machu Picchu** in the Andes of Peru.

► Soccer is the most popular sport in South America. This famous player, known as Pelé, is from **Brazil**.

◄ This man plays his guitar to entertain people on the streets of **Buenos Aires**, in Argentina. Guitar music is popular in South America.

Medellín

★ Bogotá

Cali **COLOMBIA**

**VENEZUELA**

Lake Maracaibo

★ Caracas

Orinoco River

**GUYANA**

★ Georgetown

Paramaribo

**SURINAME**

**FRENCH GUIANA (France)**

◉ Cayenne

▲ These unpolished emeralds came from a mine in **Colombia**.

★ Quito

**ECUADOR**

Guayaquil

Negro River

Amazon River

Manaus

Amazon River

Marajó Island

Belém

Fortaleza

**P E R U**

**B R A Z I L**

São Francisco River

Recife

Lima ★

Machu Picchu

Lake Titicaca

**BOLIVIA**

★ La Paz

★ Sucre

Salvador

★ Brasília

**PACIFIC OCEAN**

**PARAGUAY**

Paraguay River

Paraná River

Belo Horizonte

São Paulo

Rio de Janeiro

◉ Asunción

**A R G E N T I N A**

**C H I L E**

Paraná River

Pôrto Alegre

**ATLANTIC OCEAN**

Santiago ★

**URUGUAY**

Buenos Aires ★

◉ Montevideo

## Map Key

⊛ Country capital

◉ Other capital

• City

∴ Ruin

⋯ Boundary

| 0 | 600 miles |
| 0 | 900 kilometers |

Falkland Islands (United Kingdom)

◉ Stanley

▲ This statue overlooks the city of **Rio de Janeiro**, one of Brazil's chief ports.

# Europe

**T**ravel through the countryside in Europe and you might think you have wandered into the pages of a storybook. You'll see castles, cuckoo clocks, and cobblestone streets. But Europe is also one of the most modern continents. You can ride one of the world's fastest trains through a tunnel beneath the English Channel, watch sports cars being made in Italy, and visit famous museums in Paris. On a map Europe may look like it is part of Asia, but it is considered to be a separate continent.

Sveiks! I'm from Latvia, a country on the Baltic Sea. I am wearing a costume for a dance. Wouldn't you like to visit this town in Austria? It's on a lake high in the Alps, Europe's highest mountains.

# Europe

Iceland

## The Land

 **Land regions** Europe's most obvious feature is its coastline, cut with bays and peninsulas of every size. The Alps are high mountains that form a chain across much of southern Europe.

 **Water** Several large rivers flow across Europe. Some of the most important include the Danube, Rhine, Volga, and Rhône.

 **Climate** Warm winds from the Atlantic Ocean help give most of Europe a mild climate. This climate plus plenty of rain makes much of Europe good for farming.

 **Plants** Europe's largest forests are in the north. Cork and olive trees grow along the Mediterranean Sea.

**Animals** Reindeer are common in the far north. Many kinds of goatlike animals live in the Alps. Robins, nightingales, and sparrows are among Europe's native birds.

▶ This is a kind of wild goat called an ibex. It is one of many kinds of hooved animals that live in the **Alps** and other mountainous parts of the continent.

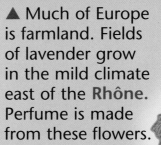

▲ People often try to climb the **Matterhorn.** It is one of the highest peaks in the Alps.

▲ Much of Europe is farmland. Fields of lavender grow in the mild climate east of the **Rhône.** Perfume is made from these flowers.

**ATLANTIC OCEAN**

Ireland

Great Britain

PYRENEES

IBERIAN PENINSULA

M

| 0 | | 600 miles |
| 0 | | 900 kilomete |

AFRICA

▶ Europe has many sandy beaches on the **Mediterranean Sea.** The most famous are along the coast, in Italy and France.

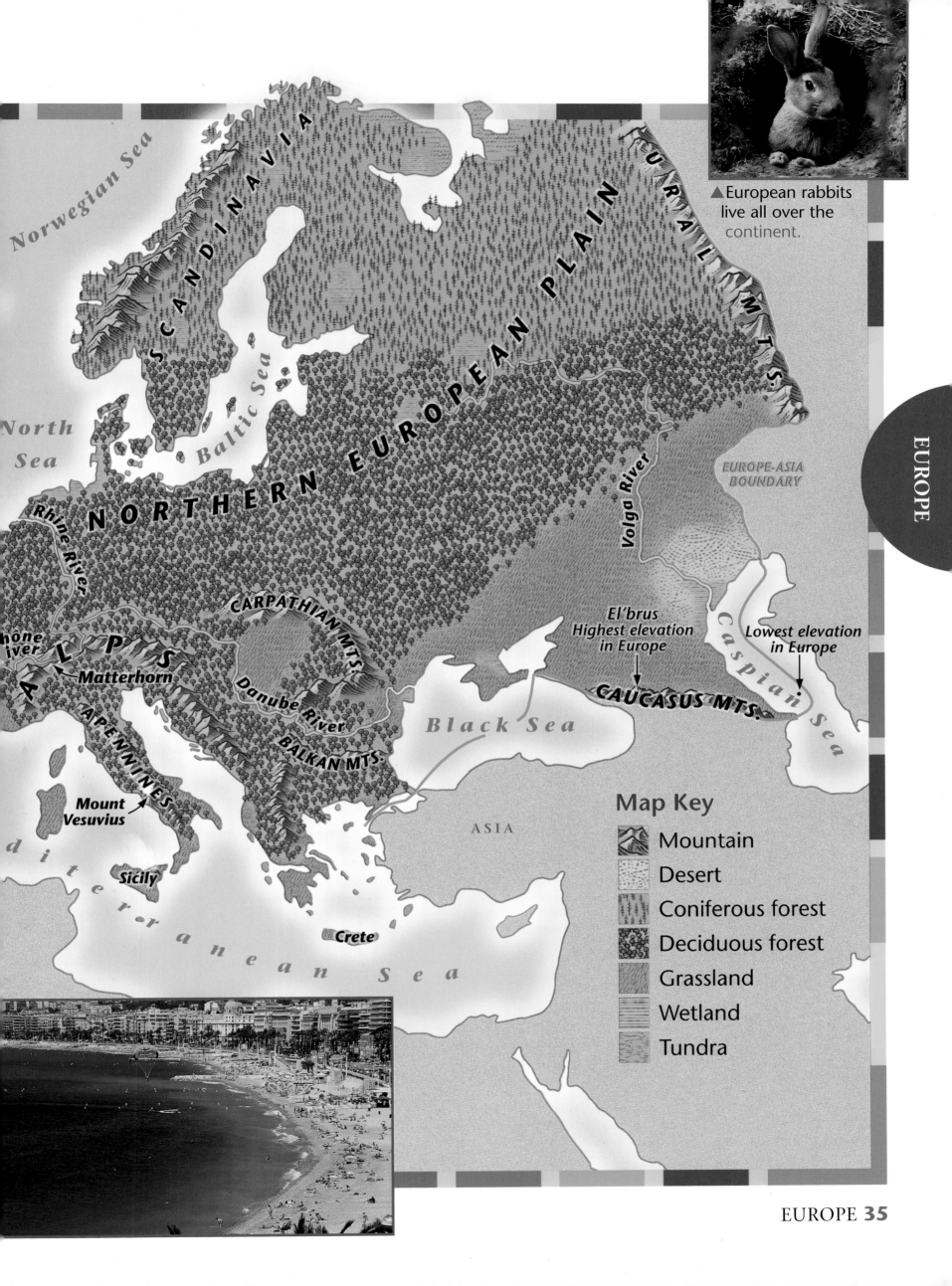

Norwegian Sea

North Sea

SCANDINAVIA

Baltic Sea

NORTHERN EUROPEAN PLAIN

URAL MTS.

Rhine River

Rhone River

ALPS

Matterhorn

APENNINES

Mount Vesuvius

Sicily

CARPATHIAN MTS.

Danube River

BALKAN MTS.

Crete

Mediterranean Sea

Black Sea

ASIA

Volga River

EUROPE-ASIA BOUNDARY

El'brus Highest elevation in Europe

CAUCASUS MTS.

Lowest elevation in Europe

Caspian Sea

▲ European rabbits live all over the continent.

## Map Key

Mountain
Desert
Coniferous forest
Deciduous forest
Grassland
Wetland
Tundra

# Europe

## The People

**Countries** There are 42 countries with boundaries entirely in Europe. Five others, including Russia, are mostly in Asia (see pages 48–49). Vatican City, Monaco, San Marino, Liechtenstein, and Malta are among the world's smallest countries.

**Cities** Most cities in Europe are within a few hundred miles of the sea. Paris, in France, is Europe's largest city.

**People** There are many different ethnic groups in Europe—usually one main group for each country. More people live in cities than on farms.

**Languages** About 50 languages are spoken in Europe, including English, French, German, and Russian. Many Europeans speak more than one language.

**Products** Europe's chief products include iron, coal, petroleum, cars, machinery, wheat, fruit, and olives.

◀ Coins called ECUs help make buying and selling easier for countries that belong to the European Union.

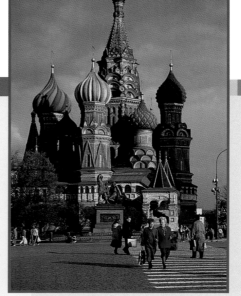

▲ St. Basil's is a famous cathedral. It is in Moscow, Russia's capital city.

▲ Bagpipe music is popular in Scotland, which was once an independent country. Today, Scotland is part of the United Kingdom.

Reykjavík ⊛ ICELAND

ATLANTIC OCEAN

Faroe Islands (Denmark)

Orkne Islana

Edinburgh

IRELAND
Dublin ⊛

UNITED
KINGDO

London ⊛

English Channel

Pari

FRA

Bordeau

ANDORRA

PORTUGAL
Lisbon ⊛

⊛ Madrid

SPAIN

Balearic Islan (Spain)

Seville

GIBRALTAR (U.K)

▼ People gather to hear the pope speak in Vatican City, the world's smallest country. It is surrounded by the city of Rome.

AFR

## Map Key

⊛ Country capital

• City

⋯⋯ Boundary

0　　　　　　　　　600 miles

0　　　　　　　　　900 kilometers

EUROPE-ASIA BOUNDARY

*Norwegian Sea*

*Shetland Islands*

*North Sea*

NORWAY

SWEDEN

FINLAND

Oslo ⊛

Stockholm ⊛

Helsinki ⊛

• St. Petersburg

⊛ Tallinn

ESTONIA

*Baltic Sea*

RUSSIA

⊛ Moscow

LATVIA

Riga ⊛

LITHUANIA

KALININGRAD (RUSSIA)

Vilnius ⊛

⊛ Minsk

BELARUS

*Volga River*

KAZAKHSTAN

DENMARK

Copenhagen ⊛

NETHERLANDS

⊛ Amsterdam

• Hamburg

Berlin ⊛

Warsaw ⊛

Brussels

BELGIUM

GERMANY

POLAND

LUX.

Prague ⊛

• Kraków

⊛ Kiev

UKRAINE

Volgograd •

*Rhine River*

*Danube River*

CZECH REPUBLIC

SLOVAKIA

Vienna ⊛

⊛ Bratislava

MOLDOVA

Bern ⊛

LIECHTENSTEIN

SWITZERLAND

AUSTRIA

⊛ Budapest

Chişinău ⊛

*Caspian Sea*

*Rhône R.*

SLOVENIA

HUNGARY

Ljubljana ⊛

⊛ Zagreb

ROMANIA

CROATIA

⊛ Belgrade

• Bucharest

*Danube River*

*Black Sea*

GEORGIA

T'bilisi ⊛

Baku ⊛

SAN MARINO

BOSNIA AND HERZEGOVINA

AZERBAIJAN

MONACO

Sarajevo •

⊛ YUGOSLAVIA

ITALY

BULGARIA

⊛ Sofia

VATICAN CITY

⊛ Rome

Skopje ⊛

*Corsica (France)*

Tirana ⊛

MACEDONIA

• Naples

ALBANIA

GREECE

*Sardinia (Italy)*

*Sicily*

⊛ Istanbul

• Ankara ⊛

TURKEY

ASIA

Valletta ⊛

MALTA

*Crete*

⊛ Athens

*Mediterranean Sea*

◀ Inspectors examine cheese at a market in the Netherlands. Europe is famous for its cheeses.

▲ These Spanish girls are dressed for a festival in Seville. Such celebrations keep folk traditions alive.

# Africa

Elephants lumber across the grasslands. Gorillas groom each other in a mountain forest. Hippopotamuses swim in a river. Amazing animals are just part of what Africa has to offer. You can also visit a busy, modern city such as Nairobi, in Kenya; see how diamonds are mined in South Africa; shop in a colorful, outdoor market; take a sailboat ride past temples on the Nile; and climb some of the world's highest sand dunes in Earth's biggest hot desert. It's called the Sahara.

Jambo! Beautiful beadwork is part of a Masai girl's traditional dress. I live in Kenya where elephants like these roam free. In the distance stands Kilimanjaro, the highest peak in Africa. You can find it on the map on the next page.

# Africa

## The Land

▲ **Victoria Falls,** on the Zambezi River, is one of Africa's wonders. Its African name means "smoke that thunders."

 **Land regions** Most of Africa is a high, flat plateau. There are few mountains. The Sahara and the Kalahari are among its largest deserts. Rain forests grow along the Equator. Grasslands cover most of the rest of the continent.

◄ Zebras live on grasslands called savannas near the **Equator.** No two zebras have exactly the same pattern of stripes.

 **Water** The Nile and the Congo are Africa's longest rivers. Most of Africa's largest lakes are in the Great Rift Valley.

**Climate** The Equator crosses Africa's middle, so many places on the continent are hot. It is always wet in the rain forest. Much of the rest of Africa has wet and dry seasons.

**Plants** Thorny trees called acacias provide food and shade for grassland animals. Date palms grow around desert waterholes. Mahogany is one of many kinds of rain forest trees.

▲ Giant sand dunes in the **Sahara** tower high above this jeep. This huge desert covers most of northern Africa.

**Animals** Some of Africa's most familiar animals are shown here. There are also lions and many kinds of antelopes. Lemurs live on Madagascar, Africa's largest island.

◄ Hot springs boil on the shores of a lake in the **Great Rift Valley.** This is actually a series of valleys that run through the eastern part of the continent.

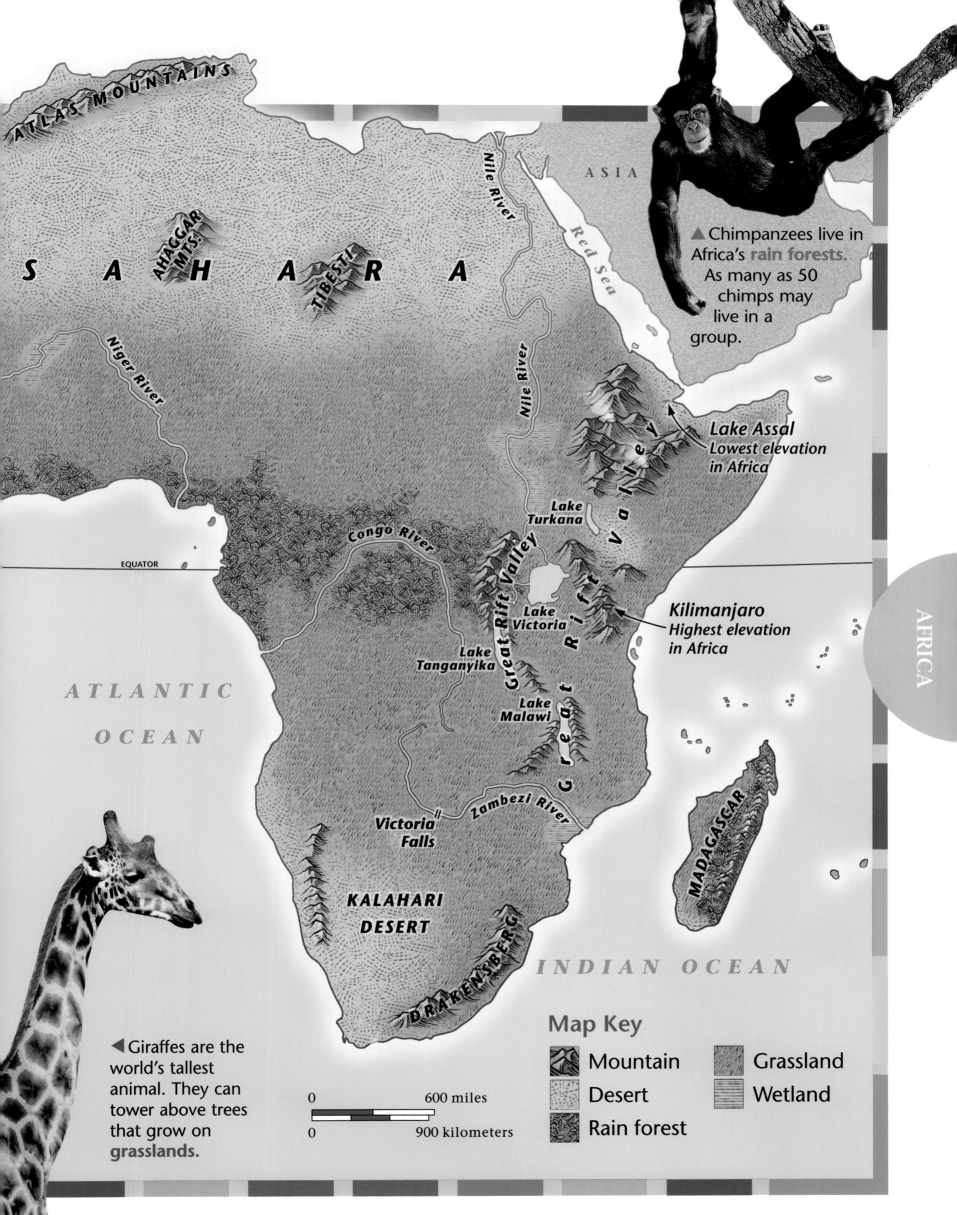

ATLAS MOUNTAINS

AHAGGAR MTS.

TIBESTI

S A H A R A

Nile River

ASIA

Red Sea

▲ Chimpanzees live in Africa's **rain forests.** As many as 50 chimps may live in a group.

Niger River

Nile River

Lake Assal
*Lowest elevation in Africa*

Congo River

EQUATOR

Lake Turkana

Great Rift Valley

Lake Victoria

Kilimanjaro
*Highest elevation in Africa*

Lake Tanganyika

Great Rift Valley

ATLANTIC

OCEAN

Lake Malawi

AFRICA

Zambezi River

Victoria Falls

MADAGASCAR

KALAHARI DESERT

DRAKENSBERG

INDIAN OCEAN

◀ Giraffes are the world's tallest animal. They can tower above trees that grow on **grasslands.**

0        600 miles

0        900 kilometers

**Map Key**

Mountain

Desert

Rain forest

Grassland

Wetland

AFRICA **41**

# Africa

## The People

◀ These boys are picking dates. **Algeria** is a leading producer of this fruit.

**Countries** Most of Africa's 53 countries were ruled by European countries from the late 1800s to the 1960s. Sudan has the most land. Nigeria has the most people.

**Cities** Cairo and Kinshasa are Africa's biggest cities. Both are on large rivers near the coast. More people live in villages and on farms than in cities.

▲ **Harare** is Zimbabwe's capital. It is one of the many modern cities in Africa.

**People** People in northern Africa's largest countries are mostly Arabs. Most black Africans live south of the Sahara in hundreds of different ethnic groups. Most Europeans live in South Africa.

**Languages** Arabic is spoken in the north. Native languages are spoken south of the Sahara. English, French, and Portuguese are the main European languages.

▲ Small sailboats called feluccas carry goods to trade along the **Nile**. This river is the longest in Africa.

**Products** Africa is a leading producer of cocoa beans, gold, diamonds, and petroleum.

▶ The Sphinx and the pyramid behind it were built by people who lived in **Egypt** thousands of years ago.

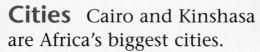

Canary Islands (Spain)

WESTERN SAHARA (Morocco)

MAURITANI

Nouakchott ✪

CAPE VERDE

Praia ✪

Dakar ✪

Banjul ✪

GAMBIA

Bissau ✪

GUINEA-BISSAU

SENEGAL

Bamako

GUINEA

Conakry ✪

Freetown ✪

SIERRA LEONE

LIBERIA

Monrovia ✪

Algiers ⊛

⊛ Tunis

⊛ Rabat
Casablanca
OCCO

TUNISIA

⊛ Tripoli

Alexandria ⦿

Cairo ⊛

ASIA

ALGERIA

LIBYA

EGYPT

Red Sea

Nile River

ALI

Niger River

NIGER

CHAD

Khartoum ⦿

SUDAN

ERITREA
⊛ Asmara

BURKINA FASO

⊛ Niamey

⊛ Ouagadougou

N'Djamena ⊛

Djibouti ⦿ DJIBOUTI

Addis
Ababa ⊛

NIGERIA

TE
DIRE
Yamoussoukro

GHANA

BENIN

TOGO

⊛ Abuja

ETHIOPIA

CENTRAL
AFRICAN REPUBLIC

idjan

Accra

Porto-
Novo

Lomé

⦿ Lagos

CAMEROON

Bangui ⦿

SOMALIA

EQUATORIAL GUINEA

SAO TOME & PRINCIPE

⊛ Yaoundé

Congo River

KENYA

UGANDA
⊛ Kampala

⊛ Libreville

GABON

DEMOCRATIC

Lake Victoria

⊛ Mogadishu

INDIAN
OCEAN

Kigali ⦿
RWANDA

Nairobi ⊛

REPUBLIC OF THE

⦿ BURUNDI

AFRICA

Brazzaville ⦿

CONGO

⊛ Kinshasa

Bujumbura ⊛

Mombasa ⦿

Victoria ⊛

CABINDA
(Angola)

CONGO

Lake
Tanganyika

TANZANIA

⦿ Dar es Salaam

SEYCHELLES

⊛ Luanda

ANGOLA

MALAWI

⦿ Moroni
COMOROS

ATLANTIC

OCEAN

ZAMBIA

Lake
Malawi

Zambezi River

Lusaka ⊛

Lilongwe ⊛

MOZAMBIQUE

MADAGASCAR

NAMIBIA

Harare ⊛
ZIMBABWE

Antananarivo ⦿

MAURITIUS
Port Louis ⊛

BOTSWANA

Windhoek ⊛

Réunion
(France)

## Map Key

⊛ Country capital
⦿ City
......... Boundary

Gaborone ⊛

Pretoria ⊛

Johannesburg ⦿

SOUTH

Maseru ⊛ LESOTHO

AFRICA

Mbabane ⦿

⊛ Maputo

SWAZILAND

Cape Town ⊛

0          600 miles
0          900 kilometers

▲ These women are
dressed for market in
**Nigeria.** Most markets
in Africa are outdoors.

▶ These students in **Kenya** study
many of the same subjects you do.
Their classes are taught in English.

AFRICA

# Asia

**A**sia is Earth's largest continent. Mount Everest, the world's highest mountain, is here. Asia also has some of the longest rivers, biggest deserts, and thickest forests. The Dead Sea is the lowest place on the continent. It is called "dead" because its water is too salty for fish and other animals to live in. More people live in Asia than anywhere else. The world's very first cities were built along river valleys in Asia long, long ago.

"Namasté!" I'm from Nepal. In mountainous countries like mine, farmers cut wide steps called terraces into hillsides to make flat land to grow crops on. Rice grows on these terraces in Indonesia.

# Asia

## The Land

**Land regions** Much of Asia is a rolling plain covered by grasslands, forests, and tundra. The Himalaya and other high mountains stretch across the south. Deserts cover much of southwestern and central Asia.

**Water** Asia has huge rivers and lakes. The Yangtze is the longest river. The Caspian Sea is the world's largest saltwater lake. Lake Baikal is the world's deepest lake.

**Climate** Northern Asia has long, icy winters and short cool summers. Most of southern Asia is warm year-round with heavy summer rains.

**Plants** Areas of coniferous forest called taiga stretch across the north. The central grasslands are known as the Steppes. Rain forests grow in the southeast.

**Animals** Tigers, giant pandas, and cobras live in the wild only in Asia.

◀ A climber stands at the top of a peak in the **Himalaya**. Mount Everest rises in front of him.

▲ A swift current carries boats through a narrow pass on the **Yangtze River**, in China.

Mediterranean Sea

Black Sea

CAUCASUS MTS.

Caspian Sea

*Dead Sea* Lowest elevation in Asia

Persian Gulf

**ARABIAN PENINSULA**

Arabian Sea

AFRICA

| 0 | 600 miles |
| 0 | 900 kilometers |

◀ Children race camels across the desert that covers most of the **Arabian Peninsula**.

▶ A herder leads his reindeer past taiga, a kind of **coniferous forest**. Forests like this are found throughout northern Asia.

ARCTIC OCEAN

Bering
Sea

EUROPE

EUROPE-ASIA
BOUNDARY

URAL MOUNTAINS

Ob River

Irtysh River

Yenisey River

Lena River

Amur River

THE STEPPES

Aral Sea

Lake
Baikal

TIAN SHAN

GOBI

Yellow River

Indus River

HIMALAYA

Brahmaputra

Ganges River

Yangtze River

Mt. Everest
*Highest elevation
in Asia*

Mekong River

Bay
of
Bengal

PACIFIC
OCEAN

South China Sea

EQUATOR

New
Guinea

Borneo

Sumatra

INDIAN

OCEAN

AUSTRALIA

▲ Boys play in a
**rain forest** in Indonesia.
These forests grow
throughout Southeast
Asia, where winds
called monsoons
bring lots of rain.

## Map Key

Mountain

Desert

Coniferous forest

Deciduous forest

Rain forest

Grassland

Wetland

Tundra

► Giant pandas live only in
leafy bamboo forests that
grow on **mountains** in
southwestern China.

ASIA

ASIA **47**

# Asia

## The People

▲ **Hong Kong** is one of Asia's busiest trading centers. It is a special province of China.

**Countries** Asia has 47 countries counting Russia. Russia and China are Asia's largest countries. Together they cover more than half the continent. Indonesia is Asia's largest island country. It stretches from Sumatra to western New Guinea.

**Cities** Much of Asia is too high, too dry, or too cold for people to live in. Most cities are near the coast or along busy rivers. Tokyo, in Japan, is the largest city.

◄ This boy in **Shanghai** draws symbols used in writing the Chinese language. Each symbol stands for a word or an idea.

**People** Asia has more people than any other continent. Each ethnic group has its own language, customs, and appearance. Most people work as farmers or fishermen.

**Languages** So many languages are spoken in Asia that even neighbors can have trouble understanding each other. India, for example, has 15 official languages!

▼ This young boy works in a spice market. In **India** people mix lots of spices together to make a strong flavor called curry.

**Products** Asia's chief products include rice, wheat, petroleum, cotton, rubber, tea, motor vehicles, and computers.

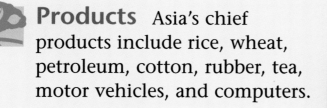

▶ This masked dancer is from Bali. Bali is one of more than 3,000 islands that make up the country of **Indonesia**.

EUROPE

Baltic Sea

RUSSIA

Mediterranean Sea

Black Sea

Istanbul

Ankara

T U R K E Y

GEORGIA

CYPRUS

Nicosia

LEBANON

Beirut

SYRIA

Damascus

ARMENIA

T'bilisi

Yerevan

AZERBAIJAN

Baku

Jerusalem

ISRAEL

JORDAN

Amman

Baghdad

Tehran

IRAQ

I R

KUWAIT

Kuwait

S A U D I

BAHRAIN

Riyadh

QATAR

Doha

UNITED ARAB EMIRATES

Abu Dha

A R A B I A

Sanaa

Y E M E N

O M A

Muscat

AFRICA

Red Sea

Persian Gulf

Ara

| 0 | 600 miles |
| 0 | 900 kilometers |

ARCTIC OCEAN

Bering
Sea

North
Land

New Siberian
Islands

Novaya
Zemlya

Sakhalin

PACIFIC
OCEAN

► Water buffaloes, like this one in **Vietnam**, are used for pulling plows in rice fields. Rice is Asia's most important food crop.

EUROPE-ASIA
BOUNDARY

Moscow

**R U S S I A**

Ob' River

Yenisey River

Irtysh River

Lena River

Amur River

Lake
Baikal

Harbin

**KAZAKHSTAN**

Astana ⊛

Aral
Sea

Ulaanbaatar ⊛

Shenyang

**JAPAN**

⊛ Tokyo
Yokohama

**UZBEKISTAN**

**MONGOLIA**

**NORTH
KOREA**

**RKMENISTAN**

Bishkek

Tashkent

**KYRGYZSTAN**

Beijing ⊛

⊛ Pyongyang

⊛ Seoul

**SOUTH
KOREA**

gabat

Dushanbe

**TAJIKISTAN**

Yellow River

Xi'an

Shanghai

**Map Key**

**AFGHANISTAN**

Kabul

Islamabad ⊛

**C H I N A**

Chengdu

Wuhan

⊛ Country capital

Indus River

Brahmaputra River

Yangtze River

Chongqing

Taipei

• City

**PAKISTAN**

Delhi

New Delhi ⊛

**NEPAL**

Thimphu ⊛

Mekong River

**TAIWAN**
The People's Republic of China
claims Taiwan as its 23rd province.

......... Boundary

Kathmandu ⊛

**BHUTAN**

Karachi

Ganges River

**BANGLADESH**

Dhaka

Hong Kong

**MACAU
(Portugal)**

Calcutta

**INDIA**

**MYANMAR
(BURMA)**

**LAOS**

Hanoi

Hainan

n

Mumbai
(Bombay)

Vientiane ⊛

**PHILIPPINES**

Manila

Philippine Sea

Bay
of
Bengal

Yangon
(Rangoon)

**THAILAND**

**VIETNAM**

Bangkok

**CAMBODIA**

Phnom
Penh ⊛

Ho Chi
Minh City

South China Sea

**ASIA**

Chennai
(Madras)

**SRI LANKA**

Colombo

Bandar Seri Begawan

**BRUNEI**

New
Guinea

**MALDIVES**

Male ⊛

**MALAYSIA**

**MALAYSIA**

Borneo

Celebes

Kuala Lumpur ⊛

**INDIAN
OCEAN**

Sumatra

**SINGAPORE**

**I N D O N E S I A**

Jakarta ⊛

Java

Bali

AUSTRALIA

► This pipeline carries oil from **Saudi Arabia** to tanker ships in the Persian Gulf.

# Australia

**A**ustralia is a most unusual place. It is the smallest and the flattest continent and one of the driest, too. It has many large deserts. "Aussies," as Australians like to call themselves, nicknamed their continent "the land down under." That's because the entire continent lies south of, or "under," the Equator. Most Australians live in cities along the coast. But Australia also has huge cattle and sheep ranches. Many ranch children live far from school. They get their lessons by mail or from the Internet or the radio. Their doctors even visit by airplane!

Awa! I'm an Aborigine, one of Australia's native people. My face is painted for a special ceremony. The giant rock behind me is sacred to my people. We call it Uluru. You might know it as Ayers Rock.

# Australia

## The Land

▲ Limestone towers rise above a **desert** in Western Australia. Desert covers much of the continent.

 **Land regions**  The Great Dividing Range stretches along the east coast and into Tasmania. Most of the rest of Australia is a plateau covered by grasslands and deserts.

**Water**  The Darling, Australia's longest river, is dry during part of the year. So is Lake Eyre, the continent's largest lake. Water lies underground in the Great Artesian Basin.

**Climate**  Most of the continent is very dry. Winds called monsoons bring heavy seasonal rains to the northern coast. Southern Australia can be cold in winter, but much of the continent is warm year-round.

▲ A school of fish swims past the **Great Barrier Reef.** It is the world's largest coral reef.

**Plants**  Eucalyptuses, or gum trees, and acacias are the most common kinds of plants. They grow throughout Australia.

**Animals**  Australia has many unusual mammals. Koalas and kangaroos raise their young in pouches on their bellies. The platypus is a mammal that has a bill like a duck's. Its babies hatch from eggs.

▲ Moss covers trees and logs in a forest in **Tasmania.** This island has a much wetter climate than most of the rest of Australia.

▶ Koalas live only in **eucalyptus forests.** At one time koalas almost became extinct. Now they are protected by strict laws.

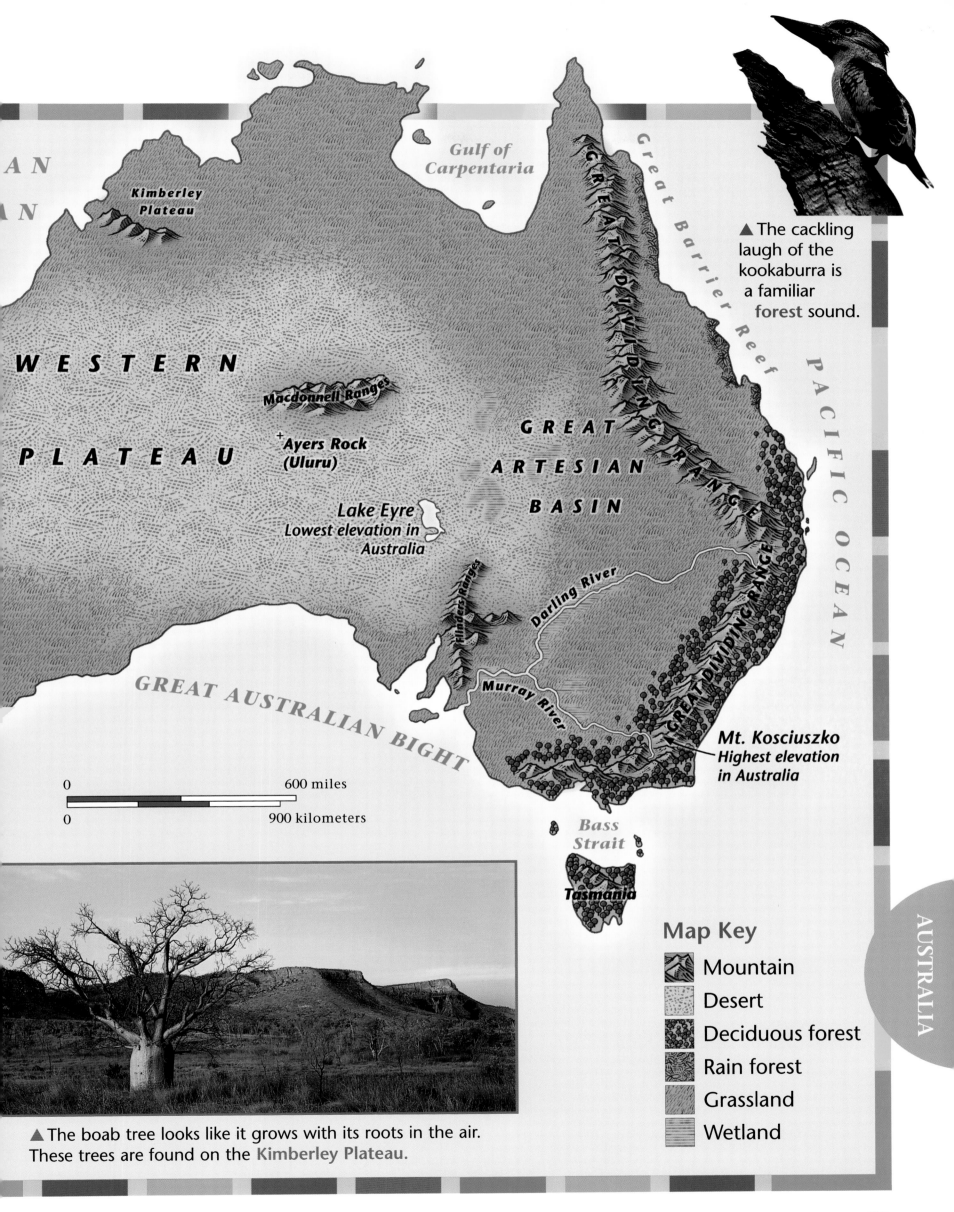

Gulf of Carpentaria

Kimberley Plateau

Great Barrier Reef

▲ The cackling laugh of the kookaburra is a familiar forest sound.

PACIFIC OCEAN

W E S T E R N

P L A T E A U

Macdonnell Ranges

⁺Ayers Rock (Uluru)

G R E A T
D I V I D I N G   R A N G E

G R E A T
A R T E S I A N
B A S I N

Lake Eyre
*Lowest elevation in Australia*

Flinders Ranges

Darling River

Murray River

GREAT DIVIDING RANGE

Mt. Kosciuszko
*Highest elevation in Australia*

GREAT AUSTRALIAN BIGHT

| 0 | | | 600 miles |
| 0 | | | 900 kilometers |

Bass Strait

Tasmania

**Map Key**

Mountain

Desert

Deciduous forest

Rain forest

Grassland

Wetland

▲ The boab tree looks like it grows with its roots in the air. These trees are found on the Kimberley Plateau.

# Australia

## The People

▲ Surfing is a popular sport in Australia. There is a city near **Brisbane** named Surfers Paradise.

 **Countries** Australia is the only continent that is also a country. It is divided into six states—including Tasmania—and two territories.

**Cities** All the chief cities are near the coast— even the capital, Canberra. Sydney has the most people, followed by Melbourne, Brisbane, and Perth.

◄ A monorail zips people around **Sydney**. The city is a busy port and the capital of the state of New South Wales.

**People** Most Australians are descendants of settlers from the United Kingdom and Ireland. Aborigines came to Australia from Asia some 40,000 years ago.

▼ Cafés, like this one, can be hundreds of miles apart in the **outback**. Few people live in this dry, central region.

**Languages** English is the main language of Australia. Aborigines speak some 250 different languages.

**Products** Australia's chief products include wool, beef, wheat, fruits, bauxite, coal, uranium, and diamonds. Most manufactured goods are imported.

◄ The world's largest cultured pearls are grown in oyster beds along Australia's **northern coast**.

*IND
OCE*

Port
Hedland

Perth

Darwin

*Gulf of Carpentaria*

NORTHERN TERRITORY

Cairns

Townsville

Mount Isa

QUEENSLAND

Mackay

Alice Springs

Rockhampton

AUSTRALIA

WESTERN AUSTRALIA

SOUTH AUSTRALIA

Lake Eyre

Brisbane

Gold Coast

Darling River

NEW SOUTH WALES

Adelaide
KANGAROO I.

Murray River

Sydney

Canberra

AUSTRALIAN CAPITAL TERRITORY

GREAT AUSTRALIAN BIGHT

VICTORIA

Melbourne

PACIFIC OCEAN

PACIFIC OCEAN

## Map Key

✪ Country capital
◉ State or territory capital
• City
......... State boundary

0            600 miles
0            900 kilometers

TASMANIA

Hobart

▲ This family lives on a farm in Queensland, where wheat is an important product.

▼ Australia has huge cattle farms called stations. Some of the largest are in Western Australia.

◄ This Aborigine is playing a wooden pipe called a didgeridoo. Many of Australia's native people live in the Northern Territory.

AUSTRALIA

# Antarctica

**B**rrrr! Antarctica takes first place as the coldest continent. It is the land around the South Pole. An ice cap two miles thick in places covers most of the land. Temperatures rarely get above freezing. It is also the only continent that has no countries. It has research stations but no cities. The only people are scientists, explorers, and tourists. Everyone stays for awhile, then goes home. The largest land animals that live here year-round are a few kinds of insects!

Chances are you'll see more penguins than people if you visit Antarctica. Like the whale behind them, Penguins depend on the ocean for food. They come ashore to have their babies.

# Antarctica

## The Land

**Land regions** The Transantarctic Mountains divide the continent into two parts. East Antarctica, where the South Pole is located, is mostly a high, flat, icy area. West Antarctica is mountainous. Vinson Massif is the highest peak.

**Water** Most of Earth's fresh water is frozen in Antarctica's ice cap. The ice breaks off when it meets the sea. These huge floating chunks of ice in the ocean are called icebergs.

**Climate** Antarctica is windy and dry. It gets very little snow. Most of the snow that falls turns to ice. The thick ice cap has built up over millions of years.

**Plants** Billions of tiny plants live in the surrounding oceans. Mosses and lichens grow on the land.

**Animals** Penguins and other seabirds nest on the coast. Whales, seals, and tiny shrimplike animals called krill live in the oceans.

▲ This strong-sided ship is an icebreaker. It cuts a path through ice in the Ross Sea.

ATLANTIC
OCEAN

▲ Few people have ever climbed Antarctica's mountains. This one is called "the Razor." It is near the coast in Queen Maud Land.

▼ Elephant seals come ashore along the rocky Antarctic Peninsula during the summer.

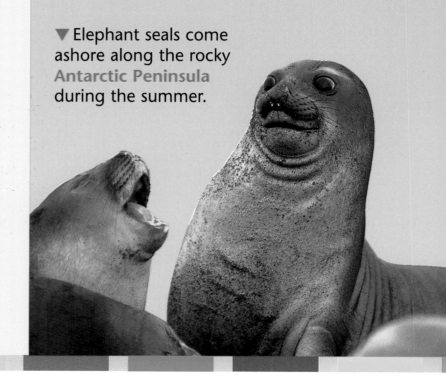

◄ Jellyfish grow very large under the sea ice around the continent. Here they have few enemies so they live a long time.

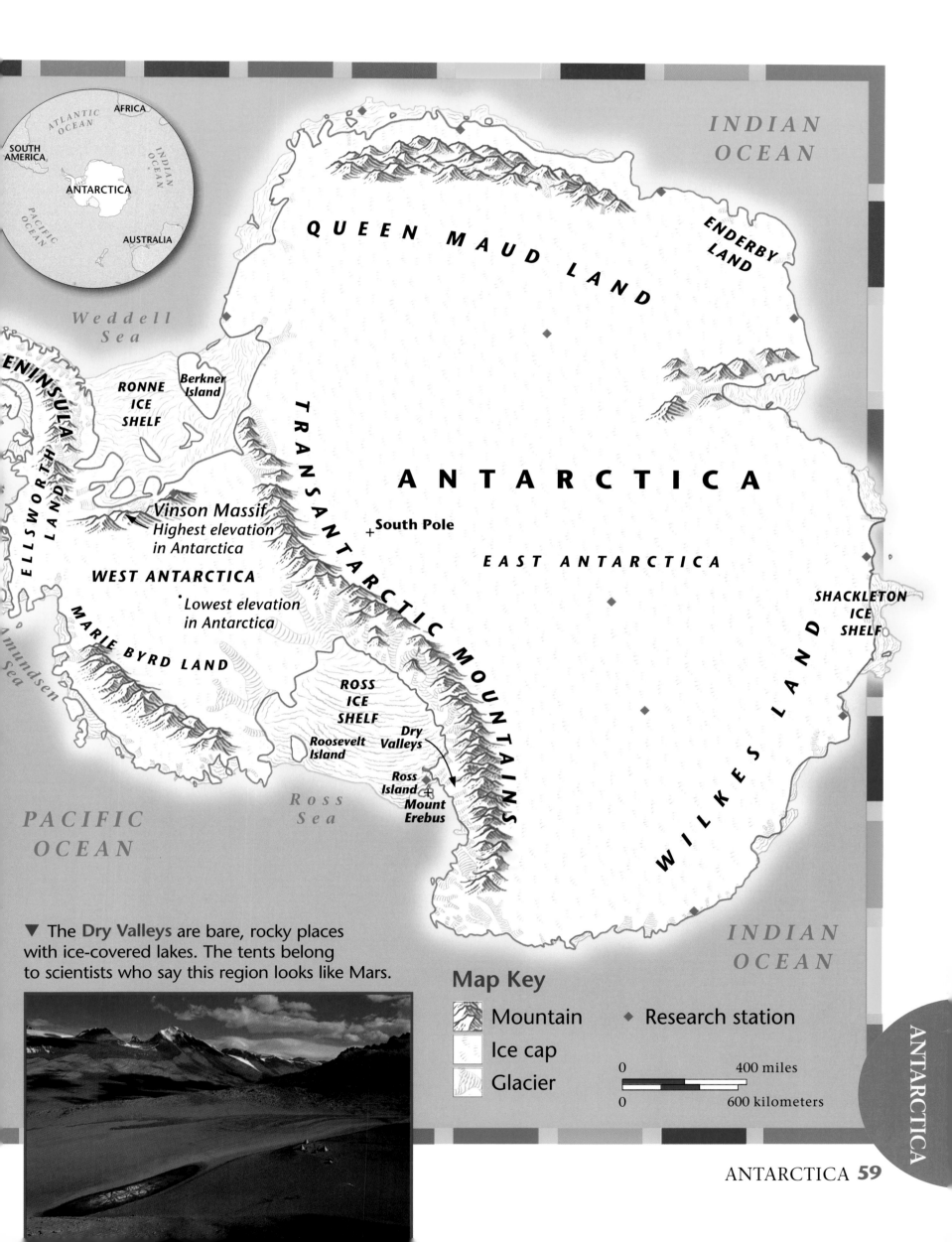

INDIAN OCEAN

ATLANTIC OCEAN
AFRICA
SOUTH AMERICA
INDIAN OCEAN
ANTARCTICA
PACIFIC OCEAN
AUSTRALIA

QUEEN MAUD LAND

ENDERBY LAND

*Weddell Sea*

RONNE ICE SHELF

**Berkner Island**

PENINSULA

ELLSWORTH LAND

Vinson Massif
Highest elevation in Antarctica

WEST ANTARCTICA

ANTARCTICA

+ **South Pole**

EAST ANTARCTICA

SHACKLETON ICE SHELF

TRANSANTARCTIC MOUNTAINS

• *Lowest elevation in Antarctica*

MARIE BYRD LAND

*Amundsen Sea*

ROSS ICE SHELF

**Roosevelt Island**

**Dry Valleys**

**Ross Island**
**Mount Erebus**

*Ross Sea*

WILKES LAND

PACIFIC OCEAN

INDIAN OCEAN

▼ The **Dry Valleys** are bare, rocky places with ice-covered lakes. The tents belong to scientists who say this region looks like Mars.

## Map Key

Mountain    ♦ Research station

Ice cap

Glacier

0               400 miles

0               600 kilometers

ANTARCTICA

# World at a Glance

## Land
### The Continents, Largest to Smallest

1. **Asia:** 17,213,300 sq mi *(44,579,000 sq km)*
2. **Africa:** 11,609,000 sq mi *(30,065,000 sq km)*
3. **North America:** 9,366,000 sq mi *(24,256,000 sq km)*
4. **South America:** 6,880,500 sq mi *(17,819,000 sq km)*
5. **Antarctica:** 5,100,400 sq mi *(13,209,000 sq km)*
6. **Europe:** 3,837,400 sq mi *(9,938,000 sq km)*
7. **Australia:** 2,968,200 sq mi *(7,687,00 sq km)*

## Water
### The Oceans, Largest to Smallest

1. **Pacific Ocean:** 64,190,671 sq mi *(166,241,00 sq km)*
2. **Atlantic Ocean:** 33,422,271 sq mi *(86,557,000 sq km)*
3. **Indian Ocean:** 28,352,382 sq mi *(73,427,000 sq km)*
4. **Arctic Ocean:** 3,662,445 sq mi *(9,485,000 sq km)*

### Highest, Longest, Largest
The numbers below show locations on the map.

❶ **Highest Mountain on a Continent**
   **Mt. Everest, in Asia:** 29,028 ft *(8,848 m)*

❷ **Largest Island**
   **Greenland, in the Atlantic Ocean:**
   840,065 sq mi *(2,175,600 sq km)*

❸ **Largest Ocean**
   **Pacific Ocean:** 64,190,671 sq mi
   *(166,241,00 sq km)*

❹ **Longest River**
   **Nile River, in Africa:** 4,241 mi
   *(6,825 km)*

❺ **Largest Freshwater Lake**
   **Lake Superior, in North America:**
   31,701 sq mi *(82,100 sq km)*

❻ **Largest Saltwater Lake**
   **Caspian Sea, in Europe-Asia:**
   143,254 sq mi *(371,000 sq km)*

❼ **Largest Hot Desert**
   **Sahara, in Africa:** 3,475,000 sq mi
   *(9,000,000 sq km)*

❽ **Largest Cold Desert**
   **Antarctica:** 5,100,400 sq mi *(13,209,000 sq km)*

## People

*Almost 6 billion people live on the Earth—enough to fill a string of school buses that would circle the Equator almost 24 times! More than half the world's people live in Asia.*

### Five Largest Countries by Number of People

1. **China, Asia:** 1,254,062,000 people
2. **India, Asia:** 986,611,000 people
3. **United States, North America:** 270,933,000 people
4. **Indonesia, Asia:** 211,806,000 people
5. **Brazil, South America:** 167,988,000 people

### Five Largest Cities* by Number of People

1. **Tokyo, Japan (Asia):** 11,573,000 people
2. **Seoul, South Korea (Asia):** 10,231,200 people
3. **São Paulo, Brazil (South America):** 10,017,800 people
4. **Mumbai, India (Asia):** 9,925,900 people
5. **Mexico City, Mexico (North America):** 8,857,500 people

*Figures are for city proper, not metropolitan area

# Glossary

**bauxite** a substance mined from the Earth that is the chief source of aluminum

**capital city** a place where a country's government is located

**city** a settled place where people work in jobs other than farming

**coral reef** a stony formation in warm, shallow ocean water that is made up of the skeletons of tiny sea animals called corals

**country** a place that has boundaries, a name, a flag, and a government that is the highest worldly authority over the land and the people who live there

**environment** the world around you, including people, cities, beliefs, plants and animals, air, water—everything

**ethnic group** people who share a common ancestry, language, beliefs, and traditions

**European Union** an organization of 15 European countries (Austria, Belgium, Denmark, Finland, France, Germany, Greece, Ireland, Italy, Luxembourg, Netherlands, Portugal, Spain, Sweden, and the United Kingdom)

**glacier** a large, slow-moving mass of ice; glaciers that cover huge areas are called ice caps

**lemur** an animal related to monkeys that is active at night and lives mostly in forests on Madagascar, in Africa

**lichen** a plantlike organism that is part alga and part fungus and that usually lives where few plants can survive

**mosses** nonflowering, low-growing green plants that grow on rocks and trees throughout the world

**outback** the name Australians use for the dry interior region of their country where few people live

**plains** large areas of mainly flat land often covered with grasses

**province** a unit of government similar to a state

**state** a unit of government that takes up a specific area within a country, as in one of the 50 large political units in the United States

**Steppes** a Russian name for the grasslands that stretch from eastern Europe into Asia

**taiga** a Russian word for the scattered, coniferous forests that grow in cold, northern regions

## Pronunciations

*Note: Syllables printed in all capital letters should be accented.*

**Aborigine**   ah buh RIJ uh nee

**Ayers**   ARZ

**Baikal**   by KALL

**bauxite**   BAWK site

**boab**   BO ab

**Buenos Aires**   bway nus AR eez

**didgeridoo**   DIH juh ree doo

**eucalyptus**   you kuh LIP tus

**Eyre**   AR

**felucca**   fuh LOO kuh

**Harare**   hah RAH ray

**Himalaya**   hih muh LAY uh

**Kalahari**   ka luh HAR ee

**Kilimanjaro**   kih luh mun JAR o

**Kinshasa**   kin SHAH suh

**koala**   kuh WAH luh

**Latvia**   LAT vee uh

**lichen**   LIE kun

**Liechtenstein**   LIKT un shtine

**Masai**   MAH sigh

**Monaco**   MAH nuh ko

**Nigeria**   nigh JIR ee uh

**Quechua**   KEH chuh wuh

**Rio de Janeiro**
  REE oo dee zha NAY roo

**San Marino**   san muh REE no

**Sudan**   soo DAN

**Sumatra**   suh MAH truh

**taiga**   TIE guh

**Tasmania**   taz MAY nee uh

**Uluru**   oo LOO roo

**Yangtze**   yang SEE

**Zambezi**   zam BEE zee

**Zimbabwe**   zim BAH bway

## Greetings in Native Languages

**awa**   AH wuh
*an Australian Aborigine word for a friendly "hello"*

**imaynalla**   ee my NAH yuh
*"greetings" in Quechua, a Native American language of South America*

**kha hay**   kaw HAY
*"greetings" in Crow, a Native American language of the United States*

**namasté**   no mo STAY
*"I salute you" in Nepalese, the language of Nepal, in Asia*

**sveiks**   SVAYKS
*"hello" in Latvian, the language of Latvia, a country in eastern Europe*

**jambo**   JAM bo
*"hello" in Swahili, a language spoken throughout East Africa*

# Index

Pictures and the text that describes them have their page numbers printed in **bold** type.

## National Geographic Society

**John M. Fahey, Jr.**
*President and Chief Executive Officer*

**Gilbert M. Grosvenor**
*Chairman of the Board*

**Nina D. Hoffman**
*Senior Vice President*

**William R. Gray**
*Vice President and Director of the Book Division*

### Staff for this book

**Nancy Laties Feresten**
*Director of Children's Publishing*

**Suzanne Patrick Fonda**
*Project Editor*

**Marianne R. Koszorus**
*Art Director*

**Carl Mehler**
*Director of Maps*

**Sharon Davis Thorpe**
*Designer*

**Susan McGrath**
*Writer*

**Marilyn Mofford Gibbons**
*Illustrations Editor*

**Jennifer Emmett**
*Associate Editor*

**Jo Tunstall**
*Editorial Assistant*

**Thomas L. Gray**
**Joseph F. Ochlak**
*Map Editors/Researchers*

**Stuart Armstrong**
**Tibor G. Tóth**
*Map Illustration*

**Michelle H. Picard**
*Map Production Manager*

**Stuart Armstrong**
**John S. Ballay**
**Tibor G. Tóth**
**Martin S. Walz**
*Map Production*

**Ann Ince-McKillop**
**Marcia Pires-Harwood**
*Text Research*

**Janet Dustin**
*Illustrations Assistant*

**R. Gary Colbert**
*Production Director*

**Lewis R. Bassford**
*Production Manager*

**Connie D. Binder**
*Indexer*

**Mark Caraluzzi**
*Director of Direct Marketing and Business Development*

**Ellen Teguis**
*Marketing Director, Trade Books*

**Ruth Chamblee**
*Marketing Manager*

**Lawrence M. Porges**
*Marketing Coordinator*

**Vincent P. Ryan**
*Manufacturing Manager*

### Consultants

**Osa Brand**
*Educational Affairs Director Association of American Geographers*

**Peggy Steele Clay**
*Teacher-in-Residence National Geographic Society*

**Jacki Vawter**
*Specialist in Early Childhood Education Alexandria, Virginia*

### Acknowledgements

We are grateful for the assistance of John Agnone, Peggy Candore, Alexander L. Cohn, Anne Marie Houppert, Sandra Leonard, and Lyle Rosbotham of the National Geographic Book Division.

The world's largest nonprofit scientific and educational organization, the National Geographic Society was founded in 1888 "for the increase and diffusion of geographic knowledge." Since then it has supported scientific exploration and spread information to its more than nine million members worldwide.

The National Geographic Society educates and inspires millions every day through magazines, books, television programs, videos, maps and atlases, research grants, the National Geography Bee, teacher workshops, and innovative classroom materials.

The Society is supported through membership dues and income from the sale of its educational products. Members receive NATIONAL GEOGRAPHIC magazine—the Society's official journal—discounts on Society products, and other benefits.

For more information about the National Geographic Society and its educational programs and publications, please call 1-800-NGS-LINE (647-5463) or write to the following address:

National Geographic Society
1145 17th Street N.W.
Washington, D.C. 20036-4688
U.S.A.

Visit the Society's Web site:
*www.nationalgeographic.com*

## Illustrations Credits

Photographs are from Tony Stone Images except where indicated by an asterisk (*)

All illustrated physical maps and accompanying icons by Stuart Armstrong

Cover globe and all locator globes digitally created by Tibor G. Tóth

**Front Matter:**
Ed Simpson 2 (top); Michael Scott 2 (bottom); Connie Coleman 3 (top left); Paul Chesley 3 (top right); James Martin 3 (center left); Art Wolfe 3 (center right); Nicholas DeVore III 3 (bottom)

**Understanding Your World:**
*Sally J. Bensusen/Visual Science Studio 4 (top art) and 5 (top left art); *Theophilus Britt Griswold 4–5 (bottom art) and 5 (top right art); *Hal Pierce: NASA Goddard Laboratory for Atmospheres, data from NOAA 6 (left); *Tibor G. Tóth 6–7 (art); John Warden 10 (left); Hugh Sitton 10 (center); Steven Weinberg 10 (left); Andrea Booher 11 (top); Greg Probst 11 (top center); *Vaughan Photography 11 (bottom center); Cosmo Condina 11 (bottom left); *Michael Nichols 11 (bottom center); Tom Bean 11 (bottom right); John Noble 14 (top left); A. Witte/C. Mahaney 14 (top right); Jack Dykinga 14 (center left); Bruno DeHogues 14 (center right); Howard Boylan 14 (bottom); Stuart McCall 15 (top left); Chad Ehlers 15 (top right); Martine Mouchy 15 (center); Mark Harris 15 (bottom)

**North America:**
Ed Simpson 16; Rosemary Calvert 16–17; Charles Krebs 18 (top); Stephen Krasemann 18 (top center); Mark Lewis 18 (bottom center); Bruce Wilson 18 (bottom left); James Randklev 18–19; Charles Krebs 19; Gary Brettnacher 20 (top); George Hunter 20 (top center); Mark Lewis 20 (bottom center); Cosmo Condina 20 (bottom center right); Nick Gunderson 20 (bottom left); David Hiser 20 (bottom right); Will & Deni McIntyre 21; Billy Hustace 22 (top); Jake Rais 22 (center); Lori Adamski-Peek 22 (bottom); Pete Seaward 23 (top); Philip H. Coblentz 23 (bottom left); *James C. Richardson 23 (bottom right); Tim Thompson 24 (top); Cosmo Condina 24 (center); Bob Handelman 24 (bottom); Chris Thomaidis 25 (top); *David Alan Harvey 25 (center); T. Davis/W. Bilenduke 25 (bottom)

**South America:**
Michael Scott 26; Tony Dawson 26–27; Nicholas DeVore III 28 (top); *James Holland 28 (top center); Bryan Parsley 28 (bottom center); Frans Lanting 28 (bottom); William J. Hebert 29; *Stuart Franklin 30 (top); Robert Frerck 30 (top center); *Heinz Kluetmeier/*SPORTS ILLUSTRATED* 30 (bottom center); Robert Frerck 30 (bottom); *Fred Ward 31 (top); Ary Diesendruck 31 (bottom)

**Europe:**
Connie Coleman 32; John Lawrence 32–33; James Balog 34 (top); Michael Busselle 34 (center); Art Wolfe 34 (bottom); Richard Passmore 34–5; *Bruce Coleman Ltd. 35; Jerry Alexander 36 (top); Yann Layma 36 (center); Michael Rosenfeld 36 (bottom left); Louis Grandadam 36 (bottom right); Maarten Udema 36–7; Anthony Cassidy 37

**Africa:**
James Martin 38; Renee Lynn 38–39; Chad Ehlers 40 (top); Kevin Schafer 40 (top center); Hugh Sitton 40 (bottom center); Michael Busselle 40 (bottom); Michael Busselle 40–41; Tim Davis 41; Will & Deni McIntyre 42 (top); Ian Murphy 42 (top center); Hugh Sitton 42 (bottom center); Sylvain Grandadam 42 (bottom); Sally Mayman 43 (top); Paul Kenward 43 (bottom)

**Asia:**
Nicholas DeVore III 44; *Gilbert M. Grosvenor/NGS Image Sales 44–45; Chris Noble 46 (top); Keren Su 46 (center); Howard Boylan 46 (bottom); James Nelson 47 (top); Paul Harris 47 (bottom left); Keren Su 47 (bottom right); Paul Harris 48 (top); Michael Ventura 48 (center); Nicholas DeVore III 48 (bottom); *Kenneth Love 48–49; Keren Su 49 (top); Wayne Eastep 49 (bottom)

**Australia:**
Paul Chesley 50; Ed Collacott 50–51; Fred Bavendam 52 (top); Stuart Westmoreland 52 (top center); Grilly Bernard 52 (bottom center); Penny Tweedie 52 (bottom); Sam Abell 53 (top); Oliver Strewe 53 (bottom); *Photo Index 54 (top); Matthew Lambert 54 (top center); Oliver Strewe 54 (bottom center); *David Doubilet 54 (bottom); David Austen 55 (top); Paul Souders 55 (bottom left); Robert Frerck 55 (bottom right)

**Antarctica**
Art Wolfe 56; Tim Davis 56–57; Kim Westerskov 58 (top); *Gordon Wiltsie 58 (center); *Norbert Wu 58 (bottom left); David Madison 58 (bottom right); *Maria Stenzel 59

**Back cover:**
Kevin Schafer (top left); Art Wolfe (top right); Masa Vemusi (bottom left); David Muench (bottom right)

Library of Congress Cataloging-in-Publication Data

National Geographic beginner's world atlas / photographs from Tony Stone Images
p. cm.
Includes index.
Summary: Maps, photographs, illustrations, and text present information about the continents of the world.
ISBN 0-7922-7502-0
1. Children's atlases. [1. Atlases. 2. Geography.] I. Title.
II. Title: Beginner's world atlas
G1021 .N39 1999 <G&M>
912—dc21

99-34652
CIP
MAPS

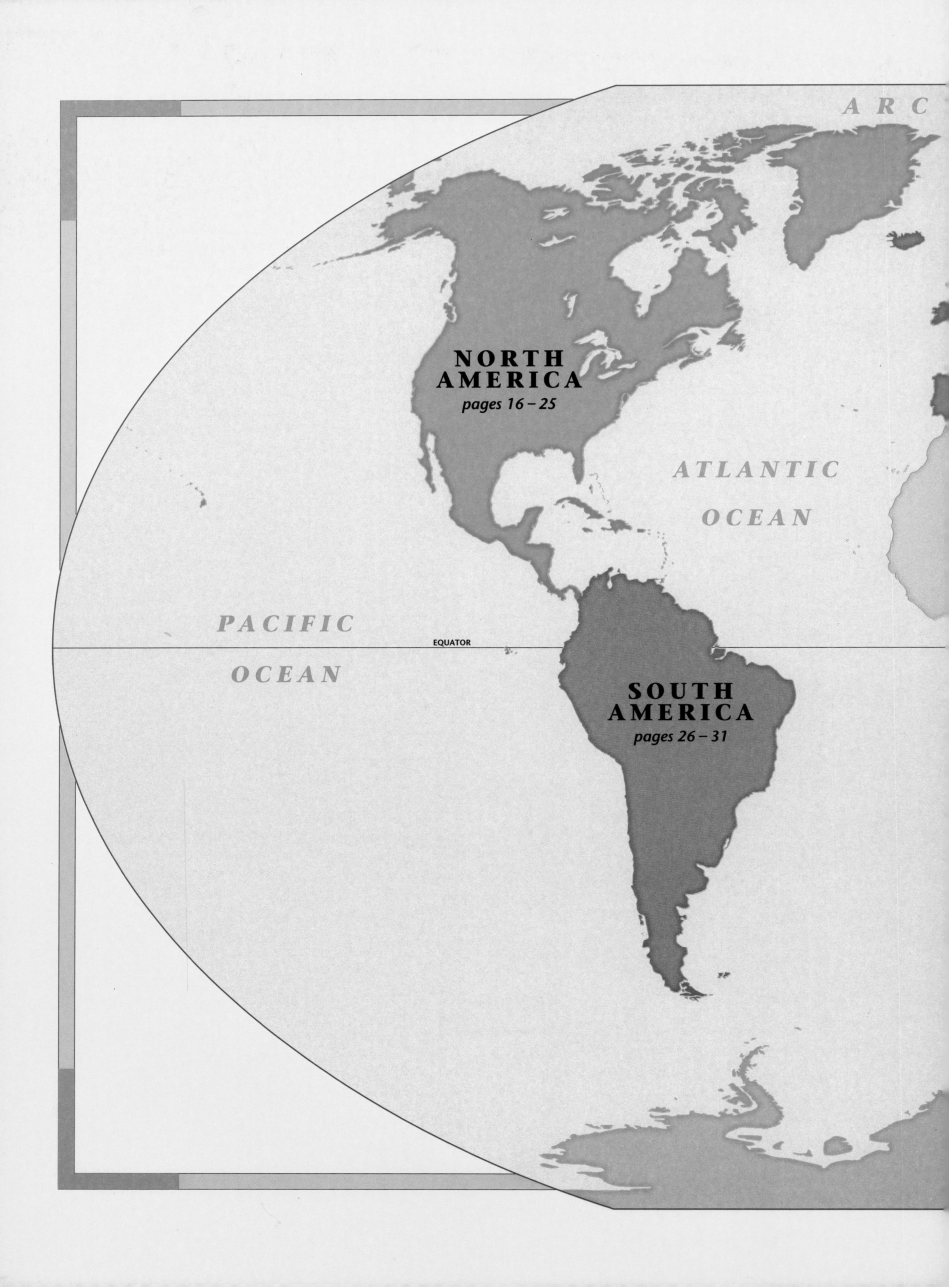

ARC

NORTH
AMERICA
pages 16 – 25

ATLANTIC

OCEAN

PACIFIC

EQUATOR

OCEAN

SOUTH
AMERICA
pages 26 – 31